**NOLO** # Products & Se...

Books & Software

Get in-depth information. Nolo publ
software programs for consumers and
download an ebook version instantly–

Legal Encyclopedia

Free at Nolo.com. Here are more than 1,400 free ... ...rs to
common questions about everyday legal i... ..s, bankruptcy,
small business formation, divorce, ...nd much more.

Plain-English Le

Free at Nolo.com ...ook it up in America's most
up-to-date sourc ...l terms.

Online Le

Create docun... ...r. Go to Nolo.... ... will
or living trust, f ...ration or obtair ...r
provisional pat...... ...ters, download ... ...ds
of high-quality ...g bills of sale, pr...
nondisclosure a... ...y more.

Lawyer Di

Find an attorn... ...Nolo's consumer-frier... ...yer
directory provi... ...les of lawyers all ove ...a. From fees
and experience ...gai ...phy, education and spe... ...ertise, you'll
find all the infor...ati... ...eed to pick the right law ...y lawyer
listed has pledged ... ...diligently and respectfully ...ts.

Free Legal Updates

Keep up to date. Check for free updates at Nolo.com. Under "Products,"
find this book and click "Legal Updates." You can also sign up for our free
e-newsletters at Nolo.com/newsletters.

13th edition

How to
Change
Your Name
in California

**Attorneys Lisa Sedano &
Emily Doskow**

Thirteenth Edition	January 2011
Editor	EMILY DOSKOW
Cover Design	SUSAN PUTNEY
Production	MARGARET LIVINGSTON
Proofreading	ELAINE MERRILL
Index	SONGBIRD INDEXING
Printing	DELTA PRINTING SOLUTIONS, INC.

International Standard Serial Number (ISSN): 1934-4503
ISBN-13: 978-1-4133-1094-8
ISBN-10: 1-4133-1094-X

Please note

We believe accurate, plain-English legal information should help you solve many of your own legal problems. But this text is not a substitute for personalized advice from a knowledgeable lawyer. If you want the help of a trained professional—and we'll always point out situations in which we think that's a good idea—consult an attorney licensed to practice in your state.

Dedication

This book is dedicated to its original author, David Ventura Loeb. David died in September 1978 in the San Diego air disaster. At the time of his death, he was practicing law in Los Angeles, specializing in problems related to the entertainment field, and had just started another book for Nolo. Over the years, even as *How to Change Your Name in California* has been frequently rewritten to reflect changes in the law, we have continued to think of it as a living memorial to David and his love of life and determination to help others. David was a good and kind man who left his friends and, hopefully, the readers of this book richer for knowing him.

Acknowledgments

Thanks to the many people who helped bring this book into being: Ken Twisselman, Suzanne Marychild, Ed Sherman, Trudy Ahlstrom, Mary-Lynne Fisher, and David Loeb's friends: Nora, David, and Darrell.

Special thanks to everyone whose time and expertise added to this book: Jake Warner, for his fine eye and tireless queries; Stephanie Harolde, for preparing copies of the manuscript; Terri Hearsh, for turning straw into gold in the production of this book; and everyone else at Nolo, whose hard work and enthusiasm add to every book.

Many thanks to Chris Daley and Shane Caya at the Transgender Law Center for their help with Chapter 7. This edition, like the one before it, has benefited greatly from the TLC's contributions to the gender change material.

About the Authors

Lisa Sedano, a former editor at Nolo, is a graduate of Harvard College and Boalt Hall School of Law. She lives and works in Los Angeles, California.

Emily Doskow is a Nolo editor, an attorney/mediator in private practice and author of *Nolo's Essential Guide to Divorce,* and co-author of *Making It Legal: A Guide to Same-Sex Marriage, Domestic Partnerships & Civil Unions* (with Frederick Hertz) and *The Guardianship Book for California,* all published by Nolo.

Table of Contents

Appendixes

Your Name Change Companion

If you want to change your name but don't want to pay several hundred dollars for an attorney, this book is for you. *How to Change Your Name in California* summarizes California law regarding name changes and provides all the forms and instructions you'll need to legally change your name in California.

Every year, thousands of people officially change their names. These are some common situations in which people seek a name change:

- **Name changes after marriage, divorce, or annulment.** A woman may legally keep her birth name when she marries or she may adopt her husband's surname—and in some states a man can now take his wife's name as well. Upon divorce or annulment, a spouse who has been using the other spouse's name may revert back to a birth or former name. A husband and wife can change their last names to a combination of the two or something altogether different. At divorce, a spouse who has kept the "ex's" last name can easily change back to a former name (or change to a new name altogether).

- **Name changes for unmarried couples.** A couple need not be legally married to assume the same last name. For example, some same-sex couples choose to use the same last name as part of demonstrating their commitment to one another. The name may be the last name of one member of the couple, a hyphenated combination of the names, or an altogether different name that the couple shares.

- **Children's names.** Often, a divorced parent with sole custody of the children wants to make sure the children have the same last name as the parent. If the custodial parent has changed her name since the marriage, she may want to change the children's names as well. Sometimes legal guardians prefer a child to have their last name. Other times, mature children have a preference for a certain name.

- **Immigrant names.** Perhaps your great-grandfather Chassonovitch changed his name—or had his name changed for him—when he came to the United States in the 1880s. As

Americans rediscover their heritages, they often want to change their last names back to their original ancestral names. Of course, there is also the reverse situation—for someone who feels no connection with a heavy six-syllable name, shortening the name or changing it altogether may be an attractive idea.

- **Lifestyle and convenience.** Why be called Rudolph, Marguerite, or MaryAnn when you feel that Glenn, Jennifer, or Penelope better expresses the real you? One Californian petitioned to change his name from Steamboat Robert E. Lee Green Leaf Strong Boy of the Wind to Robert Di Brezzio. Another who was tired of being last in every line changed his last name from Zywik to Aaron. You can be as creative as you want in selecting your name—only a few legal limitations exist on choice of name. (See Chapter 3.)
- **Name changes for transgender people.** If you have changed your sex, you may change your name to go with it, as well as your birth certificate under

some circumstances. (See Chapter 7 for more about this.)

- **Religious and political names.** Some people may wish to change their names to reflect religious or political beliefs. Famous political and religious leaders who have done this include Mother Teresa and Malcolm X. Some women feel that a birth name is an expression of a paternal heritage and decide to take on a form of their mother's name or a totally different name. For example, some women add the word "child" to their mother's first name and use this as a last name—such as Suzanne Marychild.

How to Change Your Name in California provides help for all of these situations. The steps are the same no matter what new name you choose. Whether you have a common or uncommon reason for wanting to change your name—and whether you want to use a common or uncommon name—this book will help you accomplish your goal by giving you step-by-step instructions and explaining the process from start to finish. ●

Methods for Changing Your Name

California offers its residents several relatively easy ways to change their names. This chapter gives you some background and explains the different methods.

No matter what method you use, after you officially change your name in California your new name will be valid everywhere. That's because the U.S. Constitution guarantees that the legal procedures of one state must be recognized by all.

How to Change an Adult's Name

In California, adults have always had the right to use the first, middle, and last names of their choice. The available and effective methods for changing an adult's name are:

- court petition (filing a name change petition in court), and
- other court order (obtaining a name change as part of another court proceeding, such as an adoption, divorce, or U.S. citizenship proceeding).

In years past, Californians could also change their name simply by using a different one consistently for a period of years. After explaining just below why this approach is no longer viable, we'll turn to the more effective ways of changing your name.

Usage Method

In theory, you have the legal right to change your name by the so-called "usage method," just by using your new name consistently for a period of time. Some years ago, this book wholeheartedly recommended the usage method. No question, in the past it was a great way to change your name because it involved nothing more complicated than consistently using your new name.

But today there is a strong trend to require official proof of name changes. Governmental regulations, created to combat modern types of fraud such as identity theft, are quickly making it more difficult to have a new name accepted without official documentation. No longer can you just walk into government offices, tell the clerk you've changed your name, and have your name changed in the records. This is especially true since the terrorist attacks of September 11, 2001.

For these reasons, we strongly recommend that you change your name by going to court, where you will receive a court order that serves as proof of your new name. We no longer discuss the usage method in this book, because we feel strongly that it is not a good option for changing your name.

CAUTION

The usage method is always unavailable to inmates, parolees, and registered sex offenders. Under California Code of Civil Procedure § 1279.5(a), state prison inmates, persons on parole, and those required to register as sex offenders cannot legally change their names by the usage method.

Going to Court

Petitioning the superior court to grant an official change of name is now the most widely accepted way to accomplish this task. It involves filing several forms with the court and following the other steps in the court's name change process, including publishing notice of your name change request. The result is a court order (decree) recognizing your new name. Fortunately, the forms you'll need to fill out are straightforward and the court procedures are streamlined. This book will walk you through the process, step by step. Unless you qualify to include a name change in another court proceeding, such as a divorce or an adoption, we recommend the court petition as the best way to change your name.

Under the court petition method, you will ask your local court to issue a decree officially changing your name. This is a common and simple procedure. California law requires judges to issue adult name change decrees upon request, unless

there is an important reason not to do so. Therefore, the law is very strongly on your side. Unless someone objects to your name change, it is likely the court will issue your name change decree without a hearing. (See Chapter 3.)

To use the court petition method, read this book and follow its instructions to complete the required court forms. You can use preprinted forms issued by the California Judicial Council that are contained in this book and available online. In the few relatively rare instances where additional forms are needed, we show you how to create them.

Court filing fees for a name change petition are generally between about $250 and $350. The court may waive your fees if you have a low income. (Chapter 8 has instructions about how to prepare and submit the necessary paperwork for a fee waiver.) If you hire an attorney, expect to spend upwards of $500 or more, plus filing fees, to complete the procedure. By following the instructions in this book, you can easily and successfully do the job yourself. Or, if preparing the necessary forms is too much of a hassle, you may want to hire a reasonably inexpensive nonlawyer legal document preparation service to help with the paperwork, either online or in person. (See Chapter 11 for more on how this works.)

After your papers are filled out and filed with the court, you will be required to publish a notice in a newspaper stating that you are changing your name. The newspaper will normally charge a fee of between $40 and $200, depending on the area you live in and the newspaper you choose. Once you've done this, the process is nearly complete. Unless someone objects to your name change (this is very rare), the court will likely approve your petition without your needing to attend a court hearing. Occasionally, a brief appearance before a judge is required. Either way, you can easily handle the procedure on your own following the instructions in this book.

Filing and guiding your petition through court will take a bit of time and effort. However, the court petition process is not as daunting as it may seem.

There may be another avenue available to you for changing your name. Although it still involves accomplishing a court-ordered name change, a person obtaining a divorce or annulment in California can simply ask the judge who handles the divorce to officially restore a birth or former name in the court's decree. By California law, the judge must do so upon request, even if the petitioner did not include the request in the original divorce or annulment petition. (Cal. Fam. Code §§ 2080, 2081.)

A person who is divorced in California and who did *not* ask for a name change during that proceeding can also ask the divorce court to restore a birth or former name at any time after the divorce becomes final. All you have to do is file a one-page form with the same court that took care of your divorce. If you are divorcing or were divorced in California and want to return to a former name, we

strongly recommend this procedure, which is cheaper and more convenient than other available methods. (See Chapter 4.)

Finally, if you are a permanent resident in the process of applying for citizenship, you can change your name without filing a separate petition. When you fill out the Application for Naturalization (N-400), simply enter your desired new name in Part 1, Section D of the form. Assuming you are approved for citizenship, your new name will be official after the swearing-in ceremony. (However, this option is not available in jurisdictions where the swearing-in ceremony is conducted by an immigration official rather than by a judge.)

How to Change a Child's Name

Where both parents agree, changing a child's name can be as easy as changing an adult's name. However, if the parents are at odds over whether to change a child's name, it can be difficult or even impossible. There are three possible ways to change a child's name. These are:

- **Court petition.** Petitioning a court is the most common method for changing a child's name. This process, which is fully explained in this book, is much the same as that for an adult applicant unless one parent objects, in which case a court fight may occur.
- **Adoption.** Changing a child's name during an adoption or other court procedure works well, but

is available only if you happen to be participating in the related proceeding.

- **Birth certificate.** A child's name on a birth certificate can be changed only in very limited circumstances, as discussed in detail in Chapter 5.

A Court Petition to Change a Child's Name

Both parents or one parent alone can file a name change petition on behalf of a child. Where both parents request the change, courts normally grant the request automatically. A child's court-appointed legal guardian (a grandparent, for example) can also file the petition. If the child has no court-appointed guardian, an adult relative or close friend can file the petition. Chapter 6 describes the court process in detail (for adults and children) and also contains a special section on changing a child's name when you are a legal guardian.

When one parent alone petitions to change a child's name, state law requires that the other parent be given advance notice of the proposed name change. The court will require the petitioning parent to "serve" the court papers on the other parent or to provide an explanation of why this is not possible. (This is covered in detail in Chapter 8.) If the other parent agrees to the name change in writing or doesn't respond at all, chances are good the court will approve it.

If the other parent objects to the child's name change, the court will grant the petition only if the court is persuaded that it is "in the best interests of the child." (Cal. Civ. Proc. Code § 1278.5.) In order to determine which name is in the child's best interests, the court will hold a hearing and allow each parent to state an argument. If the child is old enough, the court may choose to interview the child. (For more on the "best interests" standard, see Chapter 6.)

Changing a Child's Name as Part of an Adoption

As with an adult, a court can include a child's name change in another ongoing proceeding. For example, adopting parents often request that their adopted child's name be changed as part of the adoption order. If for some reason the court fails to change an adopted child's name, the adoptive parents may file a petition on their adopted child's behalf. In this case, the parents will use the general court petition process, and they can follow the instructions in chapters 6, 8, and 9.

Changing the Name on a Birth Certificate

In certain very limited circumstances, including typographic errors and incomplete parental information, a child's birth certificate can be changed or amended to reflect a different name.

If you are able to change a child's name on the birth certificate, the child's name is officially changed and you don't need to go to court. Chapter 5 describes the circumstances in which the state will allow a new birth certificate to be issued or an existing certificate to be amended. ●

What's Your Name?

What's Your Name?

Your name is what you go by, right? Maybe. For people who have used a number of names over the years—or are halfway through the process of adopting a new name—being able to state their own name isn't so simple. In fact, the first step in the name change process is to determine what your current legal name really is.

 SKIP AHEAD

Skip ahead if you have only used one name. This chapter helps sort out questions regarding multiple names for people who have used a number of names. If you have only used one name in your life—or are using this book to change a child's name—skip ahead to Chapter 3.

For people who have used a number of names, the following questions may arise:

- What if you've already been using your "new" name? Does that mean it's already your official name?
- What if you have more than one name? Between misspellings, nicknames, marriage, and divorce, you may have collected a string of names, with different ones appearing on different documents and IDs. How do you sort out which is your present name?

- What if you use several first names (you were born Elizabeth, used to be called Liz, and are now Lisa) and want to change all of your documents to one of those names?

There are two reasons why it's important to try to work through these and other perplexing name situations to determine what your official legal name is. First, the answer will tell you whether you need to go to court to have your name officially changed. For example, if you've been using your new name exclusively for years and especially if it appears on your driver's license, you may not need to petition a court to change your name—your new name may already be your legal name. Second, assuming you do go to court, you'll need to know how to list yourself on your court documents. The process of thinking through your current name situation will help you get a handle on all the names you've ever used and what name you will use as your present name on your court documents.

Start by making a list of all the names you currently use and what important documents each appears on. To jog your memory of every place you need to check to see how your name is listed, check out Chapter 10, where we list the most important governmental agencies and private businesses that keep track of names.

Multiple Last Names

If you have used one last name consistently for the last couple of years and it appears on most of your paperwork, including your driver's license, Social Security card, and other key documents, you won't need to go to court to adopt it. Even if this name is different from your birth name, it's now your legal name.

EXAMPLE:

When Joanne Brown was married, she took her husband's name and became Joanne Landon. Ten years later, they divorced. She decided to keep her married name. After a few years, however, she no longer wanted her husband's name. But she didn't want to "take a step back" and return to her own family name, either. Instead, Joanne coined a new name for herself—Brandon—and had all of her records changed to this name. Five years later, she worries that Brandon isn't her "official" name. Does she need to go to court? No—because she has used her new name consistently and had all her records changed, her name change is complete under the usage method. (See Chapter 1.)

Joanne was able to completely accomplish her name change without going to court, but you won't be able to do that these days. If you have used your new name for less than five years, or if you have not already been able to get all your records changed to your new name, you will need to go to court.

If you have used a number of last names over the years and your records reflect this confusion, you will need to go to court to straighten out your name situation. This is particularly likely to be true if, try as you might, you aren't able to figure out what your current legal name is. Consider the following example.

EXAMPLE:

Sidney Lakes had a terrible relationship with her father growing up and, at the age of 16, started going by her mother's family name, Becker. When she got married, she gave up the Becker name and became Sidney Loudon. A few years later she divorced and remarried, becoming Sidney Li. Sidney has always hated dealing with bureaucracies, so she never bothered to inform many of them of her frequent name changes. As a result, her wallet is filled with cards in four different names, and her filing cabinet where she keeps important documents reflects the same confusion. Sidney, who has now been Mrs. Sidney Li for five years and plans to keep that name, is ready to clean up the mess. What is Sidney's official name? If it isn't Li, does she need to go to court to make it clear that it will be?

It's not clear what Sidney's official name is—in fact, she may have more than one official name. For this reason, her best course of action is to go to court to straighten out her confused name situation. True, Sidney might be able to get all her records changed to Li without going to court, but there are three important reasons why this is not her best approach. First, a court order will clarify her name situation quickly and easily. Second, because Sidney hates dealing with bureaucracies, she'll dread the process of trying to get agencies and businesses to informally change all their records. By comparison, going to court and then using her court order to process the changes will be relatively painless. Finally, as discussed at length in Chapter 1, we don't recommend using the usage method these days.

Occasionally, the government is to blame for a person's having multiple names. Today this most often happens because a government official makes a mistake. In the past, it also frequently occurred when an immigration official or someone dealing with Native Americans arbitrarily changed a name to something more "American."

EXAMPLE:

Deer Walking On Frozen Lake was born in Oklahoma in 1962. His birth certificate lists his full name. When his parents signed up for his Social Security card, however, the bureaucrat helping them with their paperwork thought he should put the name into a more American form: Deer Frozen-Lake.

When Deer was old enough to get his driver's license, the DMV listed his name on his license as Deer W. Lake. Deer now wants to get all his paperwork in one name—and, for simplicity, he has decided he wants it to be Deer Walking. What is Deer's official name, and should he go to court?

At this point, Deer may not have just one legal name. But because his birth certificate contains all the variations of the name he wants to use in the future, he may be able to get all his records changed to Deer Walking by just showing his birth certificate. If he runs into trouble, he should go to court.

In a situation like Sidney's or Deer's, it may be difficult to figure out what your one real name is. Your best approach is to go through all your paperwork to see whether one name appears on the majority of your key government-issued documents, such as your driver's license, Social Security card, and passport. If one name sticks out, it is probably your official name. If it is on your driver's license, Social Security card, and passport, you can continue to use it. Otherwise, you will need to get a court order to change all of your important documents.

Assuming you do go to court to straighten out your personal name mess, what name do you list on your court documents as your "present" (official current) name? You should normally list either the name that is on your birth certificate or, if that name isn't on other documents you currently use (the deed to your house, your bank accounts, and your driver's license, for example), you should use the name that is on the most government IDs and records. In addition, you should list all the other names you use or have recently used as AKAs (also known as). Do this even if the name you most want to change is one of these AKAs.

EXAMPLE:

Gina's birth certificate says Gina Lopez, as do her Social Security card and driver's license. She took her husband's name when she married, becoming Gina St. Clair, but she never got around to changing her name on these important government documents. On new documents, though, she used her married name. These included the deed to her house, her credit cards, and insurance cards. Gina divorced and kept the name St. Clair. By this point, she had used the name St. Clair for ten years, and it was on all her business and personal documents. A few years later, she decided to change her name to something new: Gina Lorraine. What is Gina's official name now, and how should she list her name on her government documents?

Even though St. Clair is on more documents than Lopez, and even though Gina probably thinks of her present name as St. Clair, her official name is probably Lopez. That's because it is on her most important pieces of

identification: her birth certificate, Social Security card, and driver's license. When Gina goes to court to change her last name to Lorraine, she should list her name as: "Gina Lopez a.k.a. Gina St. Clair."

Don't worry if this AKA business seems confusing now. We'll go over it again in Chapter 6 as we help you fill out the court forms line by line.

Multiple First Names

A different situation is presented when you want to change your first name but not your last name. Government offices are generally more flexible when it comes to changing a first name. In many circumstances, you'll find that they will change your first name in their records without a court order. This is especially likely if you can show you've been using the new name. The same holds true for nicknames as well.

EXAMPLE:

Her birth certificate says "Melissa Price," but since she was a babe in arms everyone has called her Marley. Marley calls herself by this name and even got it accepted on her school documents and her driver's license. But when her parents applied for her passport, they remembered what it said on her birth certificate and listed her as Melissa. When Marley graduated from college, she decided she should use a more "mature" name. Because she liked the name Melinda more than Melissa, she asked her friends to call her that. But old habits die hard, and she still signs her name Marley half the time. Does Melissa/Marley/Melinda need to go to court to resolve the three-name confusion?

Before we can answer that question, Marley must decide what she wants her "official" name to be. Whether it's Marley, Melinda, or even good old Melissa, she should start being consistent in how she lists herself on records and IDs. After she makes her decision, she should work on getting all her records changed to her one official name. If she uses Melissa, she can probably do this without a court order, because she has her birth certificate to back her up. Marley, too, should be no problem, because she has so many documents in that name. Getting Melinda accepted by the usage method will be tougher as it's an entirely new name. But again, changing a first name is far less problematic than tinkering with a last name, so she may eventually succeed. If she wants to make her name Melinda quickly and easily, she may find that it's less trouble to go to court and make the change.

TIP

Using a nickname is no problem. One choice that Melissa/Marley/Melinda (and everyone else) has is to use one name for all business purposes and another for social interactions. For example, Walter can stick to his rather serious name for official purposes but still ask everyone he meets socially to call him Joe. It's perfectly legal.

Pen, Stage, and Other Business Names

You might be confused as to what your one official name is if you have used a pen name, stage name, or other business name for many years and have gradually begun to also use it in your personal life. These are names people have taken on for purely business purposes. For example, if a jockey named Sebastian Monkevitcz rides under the sobriquet Johnny Monk, Monkevitcz is still his name as long as he has kept it on all his personal records. Put another way, pen names or other names used for business purposes do not become your official name unless you have changed your name legally.

Therefore, if you simply want to make sure that your business name is not your official name, you won't need to go to court—so long as the name you want as your official name is the name that you currently have on your significant records. But if you want your pen name to be your official name, going to court is a good idea.

If you decide to go to court—because you want to change your name to your pen name or to an entirely different name—be sure to list your official present name on your court documents. Again, your official name is the one that is currently on all your records and government documents.

●

Restrictions on New Names

There are very few legal limits on the name you may choose. If you seek to change your name, the judge can refuse to grant your new name only if a substantial reason exists for the denial. Under California law, "substantial reasons" include the following:

- You may not choose a name for "fraudulent purposes" (meaning you intend to do something illegal using the name). For example, you may not legally change your name if your reason is to avoid paying debts, to hide from people trying to sue you, or to get away with a crime.
- You may not choose a name that will "interfere with the rights of others," which generally means choosing the name of a famous person with the intent to somehow profit from doing so.
- You may not choose a name that would be "intentionally confusing." This might be choosing a number or type of punctuation for your name (for example, "10" or "?").
- You may not choose a name that includes words that could be considered "fighting words," including threatening or obscene words, racial slurs, or other words likely to incite violence.

Unless there's a substantial reason to deny your application, such as the ones mentioned above, the judge has a duty to approve your name change.

Famous Names

Famous people, such as celebrities, politicians, and other public figures, do not have exclusive rights to their names. For example, if you look in the telephone book of a large city, you're likely to find a listing for George Bush, Michael Jordan, or Michael Jackson.

It follows that you can generally adopt the name of a famous person as long as all of the following things are true:

- You're not adopting the name with fraudulent purposes.
- You're not likely to be confused with the famous person (which could happen if you live nearby or have a similar profession).
- You will not benefit commercially or economically by using the name.
- Your use of the name will not cast the famous person in a negative light.

Some years ago, an aspiring actor with an exceptional talent for impersonating the movie star Peter Lorre petitioned the court to have his name changed to Peter Lorre. The court refused the petition when the real Peter Lorre objected to the name change. (*In re Weingand,* 231 Cal. App. 2d 289, 41 Cal. Rptr. 778 (1964).) In another case, a California resident petitioned a Los Angeles court to change his name to Jesus Christ. The court clerk made a diligent attempt to determine whether the name change was fraudulent. He found a Jesus Witness Christ living in East Los Angeles and a Jesus J. Christ in Santa Monica. It turns out that Christ is a German last name

Famous Names and the Right of Publicity

The right of publicity makes it unlawful to use another's "persona" for economic gain. For example, if you use the name or image of a famous person to advertise your product without consent, that person can sue you for hefty damages, because the famous person has the right to profit from publicizing that name. In California, this right of publicity extends to the names of famous people who have died. Their heirs have a legal right to prevent you from using the name for purposes of economic gain for years after the death of their family member. (Cal. Civ. Code § 3344.1.) Therefore, if you take on the name of a famous person, either alive or dead, you could face a lawsuit if you use the name for economic gain. Only a handful of other states have similar laws, and case law concerning these matters is contradictory.

and Jesus is a common Hispanic name. The court found no proof of fraud and approved the name change petition.

TIP

Avoid famous names if possible. Although it's true that you can choose any name, no matter how famous, as long as you don't intend to misuse the name in any of the ways discussed, it's also true that choosing

a very well-known name is likely to red flag your petition and cause a judge to question you closely. So if you want to change your last name to Greenspan, things will surely go easier if you choose Fred, rather than Alan, for your first name.

Fictitious Names

Fictitious names, such as the names of characters (Harry Potter) or companies (IBM), are almost always protected by a combination of copyright, trademark, or corporate law. If you plan to use such a name to make money or promote yourself or a product, you run the risk of a legal battle like the one a Wisconsin candidate for sheriff found himself in after changing his name to Andrew Jackson Griffith before the election. You could protect yourself by getting advance consent from the person or company with rights to the name, but this is something that rights holders will rarely give without a fat fee. In theory, you are allowed to use someone else's fictitious name as your personal name as long as you have no intent to commercialize or publicize the name (after all, lots of people are named Potter). But here again, it makes sense to modify the desired name so it is similar but not identical to the well-known fictitious name. For example, call yourself Daniel Potter or perhaps even Harold Potter, but not Harry Potter. Doing this avoids the possibility of a court fight over your intent.

Initials, Numbers, Punctuation, and One-Word Names

An initial is legally sufficient as a first, middle, or last name. The initial does not have to stand for a longer name. Well-known examples are Malcolm X and Harry S Truman. The "S'" for the former President's middle name never stood for anything—the letter itself was his middle name.

A court may use its discretion in allowing a petitioner to adopt a number as a name. For example, a man named Thomas Ritchie III failed in his court petition to change his entire name to the Roman numeral "III." The court determined that a Roman numeral is simply not a name and was inherently confusing. (*In re Ritchie*, 159 Cal. App. 3d 1070, 206 Cal. Rptr. 239 (1984).) Minnesota's Supreme Court ruled that a man who wanted to change his name to the number "1069" could not legally do so, but suggested that "Ten Sixty-Nine" might be acceptable. (*Application of Dengler*, 287 N.W.2d 637 (1979).)

A recent court decision allowed a San Diego man to add an exclamation point to his last name, and other types of punctuation have been allowed—including, of course, the ubiquitous hyphen.

California statutory law does not specifically authorize you to change your name to just one word (like "Monkeyman" or "Freedom"). But in an age where Social Security numbers and other numerical identifiers are increasingly used by governments, banks, and other important bureaucracies, and the main purpose of a name is to identify you to friends, family, and business associates, one name should be as good as two or three. And for many purposes it already is. California judges have approved one-word names on numerous occasions. The State Registrar of Vital Statistics accepts birth certificates that list only a last name for the baby. A contract signed in just one name is considered valid. The Registrar of Voters reports that they have registered people who changed their names by court petition to just one name (especially rock stars).

Many other states agree that if you want your only moniker to be "Moniker," that's okay. For example, in the Missouri case of *In re Reed*, 584 S.W.2d 103 (1979), an appeals court allowed a petitioner to change his name to "Sunshine."

> **TIP**
>
> **Adding just one initial makes a one-word name work.** Practically, you will run into hassles if you only use one name. Every form you fill out requests at least two names, and many computers have trouble fathoming single names. You'll also likely run into resistance from at least some bureaucrats who think having just one name is not acceptable. But if you try using one name and find that it's too much trouble, you can make even the fussiest computer happy by adopting a single initial for your first or last name. For example, just plain George could become O. George or George O.

Racial Slurs, Fighting Words, and Other Forbidden Names

You may not use the court petition method to adopt a name that includes a racial slur or other words that offend others so intensely that they are likely to respond with violence. An African-American educator from Thousand Oaks, California attempted to change his name to "Misteri Nigger" (pronounced "Mr. Nigger"). By using this name, he hoped "to steal the stinging degradation—the thunder—from the word nigger," and thus "to conquer racial hatred." Nevertheless, the court ruled that a racial epithet—that is, a disparaging or abusive word that may be a "fighting word"—may not be adopted by the court petition method. (*Lee v. Ventura County Superior Court*, 9 Cal. App. 4th 510, 11 Cal. Rptr. 2d 763 (1992).) So, regardless of your intentions in choosing a new name, a court may deny it if it is an ethnic or racial slur or includes words of threat or profanity.

But can you change your name to something like "Pregnant Chad" or "Merri Christmas"? That depends on the particular judge, who has discretion in deciding whether to grant a name change. In theory, both of these should be fine—they aren't profane and don't constitute an ethnic or racial slur. Of the two, Pregnant Chad is more problematic because some judge with no sense of humor and a long memory might say it amounts to fighting words. But what about Merri Christmas? At least one judge has already approved it.

Of course, you can always appeal the judge's decision. This process involves taking your case to the California Court of Appeal. Doing this will be time-consuming and, if you hire a lawyer, expensive. Because it is almost never done, we do not cover the appeals procedure in this book.

Titles and Forms of Address

A title or form of address, such as Mr. or Ms., is not considered part of a legal name. You are allowed to use whatever title or form of address you like, regardless of age or marital status. You are also free *not* to use any title if you don't want to. For example, a married woman is free to use Miss, Ms., no title at all, or the more traditional Mrs.

Only one limit exists in using titles: You cannot use a particular title in an attempt to commit fraud, such as to appear married when you are not. The same holds true for professional titles, such as Dr., M.D., Esq., or J.D. You cannot use any of these titles in a way that implies you are a licensed physician or attorney if you are not.

A judge might deny your name change request if you wanted to change your first name to a title. For example, the name Mrs. Smith might be considered inherently confusing, especially if a man wanted to use this name. A court might allow a name such as Doctor Jones, but not if it found the public would be confused into believing the person was actually a doctor.

Names You May Give a Child at Birth

In this country, it is common for children to take their father's last name. This is a customary practice; it is not required by law. Customs vary in other countries. In many Spanish-speaking countries, a child's last name is a combination of the mother's and father's last names. In medieval France, it was common practice for girls to take their mother's last name and boys to take their father's last name.

In California, you can legally give your children any last name you wish, so long as it does not violate any of the restrictions described in this chapter. For example, parents could give their child:

- the mother's last name
- the father's last name
- a combination of both last names (for example, Duffey-Loeb), or
- a last name that is totally unrelated to either of the parents. For example, several decades ago actress Jane Fonda and her political activist husband, Tom Hayden, named their son Troy O'Donovan Garity.

Children's Names and Paternity

Giving a child a certain man's last name does not make the man the legal father of the child, nor does it make him legally responsible for the child. Paternity (the legal recognition of fatherhood) and names are two completely different legal animals. It is always a mistake to give a child the last name of a man who is not the true father because you hope it will get him to assume parental and financial responsibility. It will not make him legally responsible for the child unless he currently is your husband, and later you will have a hard time getting the name changed on the birth certificate.

When you have a child, a hospital worker or the person who delivered the baby is legally required to complete the birth certificate with information that you give him or her and then file it with the state. Before you sign the completed birth certificate, make sure the child has the name you've chosen and that all the information is correct. As we describe in Chapter 5, birth certificates are very hard to change.

Marriage, Divorce, and Custody

Marriage and divorce are the two most common reasons why adults change their names. In both cases, the main rule is simple: Whether you change your name is entirely up to you. A woman who marries may adopt her husband's last name, keep her birth name, or even create a new name. The same goes for men. Today it's not as unusual as it once was for newly married men to change their names to reflect their new union rather than continue to use their family name, but as you'll read below, currently it's easier for women than for men to change their name upon marriage.

At divorce, the same options exist: A spouse has the choice of keeping a married name or returning to a birth or former name. Over time, women (or men) may change their names a number of times. For example, a woman might take her husband's last name when she marries, resume her birth name when she divorces, and change to her new husband's last name when she remarries.

TIP

"Birth name" = "maiden name." Traditionally, the family name a woman was born into was referred to as her "maiden name." But way back in 1974, the California legislature changed maiden name to "birth name" in many of the more important laws dealing with names. For this reason, the term birth name is used in this book and, when dealing with the legal system, should be preferred to maiden name. In situations where a divorcing person wants to reassume the name of a previous spouse, the term "former name" is most appropriate.

Marriage

People who marry are free to keep their own names, adopt one spouse's last name for use by both, hyphenate their names, or choose a completely new name. In many Western countries, women have traditionally taken their husband's family name. Women are free to keep their own family names, though, and many women do. Other naming options exist for married couples. For example, a couple could adopt a combination of their last names, either hyphenated (Ellis-Manning) or merged (Ellman). Or, they can pick an altogether new and different last name.

Keeping Your Name When You Marry or Register as Domestic Partners

There is no law in California that requires a woman to assume her husband's name upon marriage—and today many choose not to. Likewise there is no requirement that registered domestic partners share the same name.

By law, a woman cannot be discriminated against in businesses or credit matters because of her name. California law requires that all businesses accept a married woman's birth or former name if she regularly uses it, regardless of her marital status. (Cal. Civ. Proc. Code § 1279.6.) The law also requires credit card companies to issue credit cards in the name a woman requests, be it her birth name or married name. However, the credit card company is allowed to insist that a married woman establish an account separate from her husband's. (Cal. Civ. Code § 1747.81.)

Look Up the Law

How to look up the law. All California laws can be read free of charge in the legal research area of Nolo's website at www. nolo.com/legal-research/state-law.html.

If you want to keep your name when you marry or register, simply don't change it. There's no need to file any documents with the court, because a married person only acquires a spouse's name if the person chooses to. Just don't use your husband's or partner's name, and keep your own name on all records.

It makes little sense to notify agencies and businesses you deal with that you got married but don't want your records changed. You will only risk confusing people. It's possible that some of your records may get changed to your spouse's name when the news of your marriage filters through the bureaucracy. If so, you will have to contact someone about changing those records back.

It's not uncommon for women who are or have been married to use more than one name. For example, a newly married woman may change some of her records to her new married name while leaving others in her birth name. Women who don't consistently use the same name are bound to run into occasional confusion and inconvenience. For example, a woman with a bank account in her birth name may run into trouble if she tries to cash checks with an ID showing her married name. She'll probably need to supply a copy of her marriage license or a piece of convincing ID that still shows her birth name.

A Historical Note: "Lucy Stoners"

Over the years, many married women have retained their birth names. Pioneering American suffragette Lucy Stone began the tradition in 1855, when she created a furor as the first American woman to keep her name after marriage. In Stone's honor, Ruth Hale, a New York journalist, founded the Lucy Stone League in 1921. A "Lucy Stoner" is now defined in many dictionaries as "a person who advocates the keeping of their own names by married women." Some of the early Lucy Stoners included Amelia Earhart, Edna St. Vincent Millay, and Margaret Mead.

Changing Your Name When You Marry or Register as Domestic Partners

Until recently, it was customary in our society for a woman to adopt her husband's last name when she married. Though the custom may be eroding, or at least losing its pervasiveness, it is still very common for women to take their husband's names. People (even bureaucrats!) usually accept the new name without a hassle because the practice is so widely followed. Sometimes they'll even throw in a smile and a "congratulations." Because this type of name change is so accepted, it is one of the few types of name changes that can be done without a court order.

In the past, it's only been brides who were subject to this special ease in officially changing their names. This year, it appears the Legislature is catching up with the times. But a new law allows either party to a marriage (or registered domestic partnership) to change to a different name without a court order as long as the new name fits in one of the following categories:

- the current last name of the new spouse or domestic partner
- the last name of either spouse or domestic partner given at birth
- a name that consists of a combination of all or a part of either or both partners' current last names or last names given at birth, or

- a hyphenated combination of the spouses' or partners' last names. (Cal. Fam. Code § 306.5.)

If you both want to change your names to an entirely new shared name that has no connection to any name either of you has ever used, you'll still have to go to court for that.

Currently, same-sex married couples and domestic partners can sometimes run into trouble with the DMV when trying to get their names changed after registering. Although the DMV website says that domestic partners can take each other's names by showing a registration form alone, couples have reported that some clerks have been less than cooperative with efforts to obtain a new driver's license this way. Also, California domestic partner registration is recognized only within the state (and in some of the other states that acknowledge same-sex relationships). The name change made on that basis may not be recognized by the State Department for purposes of changing your passport, or the Social Security Administration for purposes of changing your Social Security card. While the new law will require the DMV to change your drivers' license after you register as domestic partners, it may still be problematic to get a new Social Security card—forcing you to go through a court process anyway.

Returning to Your Birth or Former Name While Married

Over time, the name you use after marriage will appear in more and more records—your driver's license, tax returns, and credit cards, for a start. You can save yourself considerable trouble later by making sure you are happy using your spouse's name before you have any records changed. After making the change, a number of women wish they had instead kept their birth name. But after years of usage, many conclude it's too much trouble to readopt their birth name.

California courts have upheld the right of women to retain or return to their birth or a former name, and routinely grant married women's petitions to return to their birth names. In analogous court cases, it has been held that a married woman may be sued in her birth name, and a wife's last name does not automatically change when her husband changes his name, unless she consents. (*Sousa v. Freitas*, 10 Cal. App. 3d 660, 89 Cal. Rptr. 485 (1970).)

If you are married and you go to court to change your name to a name other than your husband's, on rare occasions a male judge may ask whether your husband agrees with the change. The law does not require your husband to cosign the petition or attend the hearing (in the unusual case that the court holds a hearing). But, your husband is free to do so, and for personal reasons you may want him to. But if it is important to you

to make the change on your own (even over the objections of your spouse), there is nothing in the law to stop you.

If you return to your birth (or a former) name, be prepared to deal with the fact that some agencies or credit granters may wrongly conclude you have divorced. As part of the process of notifying them of your new (old) name, you'll want to make it clear that no divorce is involved.

Divorce and Annulment

Women completing a divorce or annulment have the same options for their name as they did when they got married. If they have taken their husband's last name, divorcing women are entitled to keep that name. They can also return to a birth name or to a former name from a previous marriage—as can men who have taken their wives' names, and same-sex spouses or domestic partners if one took the other's name. Each woman facing divorce can make this choice for herself. If she has children from the marriage, her ability to keep or change her name isn't affected by who has custody or what last name the children have. Because the same rules govern divorce and annulment, for the sake of brevity throughout the rest of this section we refer only to divorce.

If a woman decides to keep her husband's name, she can continue to go by the first and last name of her ex-husband— for example, "Mrs. Robert Smith"—if she chooses to. The only exception to this rule is that a divorced woman may not use her married name fraudulently. For example, she cannot use the name in order to falsely pass herself off as still married to her ex-husband or to avoid creditors.

Many women who are divorcing choose to change their names. Often, they want to return to their birth name or to a name from a previous marriage. California law has created an easy way for women (and men) who are divorcing (or who have divorced in California) to officially return to a former name. You can use this procedure if you are in the midst of a divorce, or you can use it after the divorce is final.

> **CAUTION**
>
> **These rules do not apply to legal separation.** If you are separating from your spouse but not divorcing, you will have to file a court petition to change your name.

Returning to Your Former Name— During the Divorce Proceeding

If you are divorcing (or having your marriage annulled) in California, the Family Code makes it easy for you to return to your birth name or a former name. At any time during the divorce proceeding, you can ask the court to restore your name. Under Family Code sections 2080 and 2081, the court is bound to grant your request and file a formal order restoring your birth or former name.

The statute is clear that you don't have to make the request in your original divorce petition. Instead, you may make your request in a separate petition in the same action, at the divorce court hearing or at any time after the divorce is final. (See below for instructions on restoring your name after the divorce is final.)

Once the court orders that your name is returned to your former name, your name change is complete. The court order is all the paperwork you'll need to have your name changed in other records.

Returning to Your Former Name— After the Divorce Proceeding

If you decide after your divorce to give up your married name and return to your birth name or other former name, there's an easy way to do it if the divorce took place in California. You can accomplish the change by filing one straightforward form with the same court that processed your divorce. Called an Ex Parte Application for Restoration of Former Name After Entry of Judgment and Order, this is a simple one-page form.

> **CD-ROM**
>
> You'll find a blank Ex Parte Application for Restoration of Former Name After Entry of Judgment and Order on the CD-ROM at the back of the book. You can also download the form or fill it out online at www.courtinfo.ca.gov/forms/fillable/fl395.pdf.

Here are instructions for filling out the Ex Parte Application.

Caption. The box at the top of the page is called the caption. Fill in the caption boxes with the exact case name and number from the divorce or annulment proceeding. Pull out your divorce paperwork to be sure you've got it right. The only thing that might be different is the top left box, where you enter your name. If you had an attorney represent you in the divorce or if your address has changed, this will be different. Enter your name, address, and telephone number here. Where it says "Attorney for:" put "In pro per," which means you are representing yourself.

Item 1. This line asks for the date your divorce or annulment became final. Fill in the date the court entered the final order.

Item 2. List the name you want to return to on this line.

Date and Signature. Write the date and your current (married) name, not the name you are petitioning to return to. Sign the signature line with your current name.

You are not required to send a copy of the application to your former spouse. Just fill out the application, file it with the divorce court, and pay the filing fee. After the judge signs the form, your name change is complete. A copy of the order is your proof that your former name has been restored.

Using the Usage Method to Return to a Former Name

Because women often return to their former names after divorcing, they could traditionally make this change using the usage method without going to court. However, DMV regulations have called this into question. The regulations require an applicant to produce official proof of a name change. Acceptable proof includes a divorce order *that lists the legal name of the applicant as a result of the proceeding.* So, if you didn't have the divorce court change your name, the DMV won't change your name on your driver's license or ID card. That's why we suggest you petition the divorce court to legally change your name. (This might be different if you were divorced outside of California; see below.)

TIP

You may be able to change to a new name at divorce. The simple name change at divorce procedure described in the California Family Code refers only to birth or former names. This means that if you want to change your name to an entirely different name during or after your divorce, the court may not grant your change, because it is not required to do so. But if your divorce is not yet final, you may as well try asking the court to change your name—even if you want an entirely new name. If the court refuses to grant it, you can just file a separate name change petition (following the instructions in Chapter 6).

In some circumstances, a person who is divorced may not be able to use the divorce process to accomplish a name change. For instance, you may have been divorced in a state other than California.

Custody, Remarriage, and Children's Names

When parents split up, their children's last name can often become an issue. One common conflict arises when a woman who has taken her husband's name gets custody of the children. If she returns to her birth name or former name, she may want her children's last name to match hers. Or, if she remarries and takes her new husband's name, she may want her children to bear the name of her new husband.

If the child's father consents to a proposed name change, the court should grant the change without batting an eye. When both parents support a child's name change, the court will normally grant it, regardless of whether the parents are married to each other. It is a different matter, however, when one parent contests the name change. Typically, a father who continues to support and care for his child will want the child to continue to bear his name even if the child's mother feels differently.

Traditionally, courts used to find that a father had an automatic right to have his children keep his last name if he continued to actively perform his parental role. No longer. Today, there are no automatics—instead, court decisions regarding children's names turn on "the best interests of the child." In some instances, a court may also consider whether the parents had a preexisting agreement about the child's name. The court will look at all the factors in each particular case and listen to all the parties involved. What this all boils down to is that it's up to a judge to decide which name is in the children's best interest. We discuss the "best interests" standard in Chapter 6.

Giving a child a different name from the father's or otherwise changing the child's name does not affect the parent-child relationship in the eyes of the law. For example, if you change your child's last name to your new husband's name, your new husband does not become the child's legal father. Names do not affect what the law calls "paternity" (the legally recognized identity of the child's parents).

The new husband of a woman with custody of her children cannot petition to change the children's names unless he has legally adopted them (in which case the name change can be easily done as part of the stepparent adoption). Normally, a stepparent can adopt a spouse's child only with the consent of the child's other parent, if the other parent has abandoned the child (not visited or provided support for the child in over a year), or if the other parent has passed away.

A child's name change also does not affect the rights or duties of either parent, including visitation, child support, or rights of inheritance. Only a court proceeding that changes who the child's legal parents are could make such a change. Such proceedings include a legal adoption or a hearing to establish the father's identity—not a name change petition.

Although you may be able to change your own name in a divorce proceeding, you will not be able to change your child's name in the divorce proceeding. If you want to change your child's name, you'll have to file a separate court petition. For more information on how to change your child's name, see chapters 1 and 6. ●

Birth Certificates

When a child is born, hospital personnel or the person who delivered the baby outside of a hospital completes a birth certificate to register the birth officially. A birth certificate normally lists the child's name, the names of the child's parents, and the time and place of the birth. The State Registrar of Vital Statistics keeps original birth certificates after they have been reviewed by the local health department. County health departments maintain copies of birth certificates for births in the county during the last year or two; county recorders maintain copies for all births in the county.

In rare circumstances, described below, a child's name can be changed by having a birth certificate amended or issued in the new name. In a few instances, a new birth certificate can be issued, and, in others, you can receive an official amendment with new information that can be attached to the existing birth certificate.

The Office of Vital Records usually will not issue a new birth certificate for an adult. If an adult wants a court-ordered new name reflected on a birth certificate, that person will have to settle for an amendment that can be attached to the existing birth certificate. See "Adults and Birth Certificates," below, for more information.

CAUTION

Only California birth certificates are covered here. This chapter describes the law of birth certificates for people born in California. If you were born in another state or country, contact that state's vital statistics department for information on changing your birth certificate.

Birth Certificates and Names Are Two Different Things

If you change your name, you do not need to change or amend your birth certificate to complete the process. In fact, in most name change circumstances, you won't be allowed to change your birth certificate. But even when people are able to change or amend their birth certificates to reflect a different name, doing so is a separate bureaucratic process from the name change itself. The only exceptions to this rule relate to children and are described below, in "Children and Birth Certificates"; in these narrow circumstances, a child's birth certificate can be changed to reflect a new name. This action also officially changes the child's name.

Children and Birth Certificates

There are several circumstances under which a minor child can get a totally new birth certificate and have the old birth certificate sealed so that it can only be accessed by a court order. In other situations, an existing birth certificate can be amended to add new information through an attachment. This section describes all the ways that a child's birth certificate can be changed.

Adding a Father's Name Through Acknowledgment of Paternity

When a child's birth certificate lists only a mother, you can add a biological father's name to the birth certificate by filing a form called an Application to Amend a Birth Record—Acknowledgment of Paternity (VS-22). You can get this form from the Department of Health Services, Office of Vital Records (OVR), or at your local county recorder's office. The contact information for the Office of Vital Records is listed at the end of this chapter, in the section titled "Forms and Assistance From the OVR." The OVR forms are not available online, but you can order them online, as described in that section. The OVR also provides information pamphlets that are available online and that explain the entire process in detail.

In the Acknowledgment of Paternity form, both the mother and the biological father acknowledge the child's paternity

and request that a new birth certificate be issued. The Acknowledgment of Paternity form must be accompanied by one of two types of documentation, depending on whether the parents were or are married to each other:

- If the parents were married at any time after the child's birth, the parents submit a copy of the marriage certificate and a notarized sworn statement in a form provided by the Office of Vital Records, along with the Acknowledgment of Paternity form.
- If the parents were never married, then both parents will have to sign a form called a Voluntary Declaration of Paternity, and submit it with the Acknowledgment of Paternity form. The Voluntary Declaration of Paternity must either be witnessed by a county welfare worker or a staff member at the district attorney's family support unit, or notarized by a notary public. The Voluntary Declaration of Paternity form is available through the California Department of Child Support Services website at www.childsup.cahwnet. gov (click the link for the "Paternity Opportunity Program"), at the Family Support Section of any district attorney's office, or from your local county registrar of births and deaths.

When you submit these forms, you can also request that the child's last name be changed to match the last name of the father. You can also add a first or middle name, if there is none currently listed on the birth certificate. However, you can't change a first or middle name this way.

After the child's birth certificate has been changed, the original birth certificate will be sealed, and can be accessed only with a court order.

This process works only if no one was listed as the father on the original birth certificate. If a man wants to acknowledge his paternity of a child but the child's birth certificate already lists another man as the father, the second man can't use this simplified procedure. Instead, the second man would have to initiate a paternity lawsuit in order to have the birth certificate changed. We describe this process next.

Changing a Father's Name on the Birth Certificate Through a Judicial Decree of Paternity

A "paternity action" is a lawsuit to determine the father of a child. Such a lawsuit can be brought to court by the father, the mother, or a district attorney. Many paternity actions are initiated by district attorneys on behalf of county welfare offices that provide financial assistance to families and are required by law to seek reimbursement from the father. If a court finds a man to be a child's father, the man will have a legal duty to support the child. His visitation rights and the child's rights to inherit are also affected.

SEE AN EXPERT

If you need to establish paternity in order to put a biological father's name on a birth certificate, you will probably want to consult a lawyer. See Chapter 11 for more information about hiring a lawyer.

If the court determines that a certain man is the father, it will issue a "judicial decree of paternity" or an "adjudication of paternity"—an order officially declaring this fact. With a judicial decree of paternity in hand, the father or mother can request that a new birth certificate be issued containing the relevant information. (Cal. Health & Safety Code §§ 102725–102735.) The form to use for this process is called Application to Amend a Birth Record—Adjudication of Facts of Parentage (VS-21), and it's available from OVR or your local county recorder, as described at the end of this chapter.

If another man was previously listed as the father on the original birth certificate, his information will be removed and replaced. At this time, the child's last name can also be changed on the birth certificate to that of the man declared to be the father, as long as the court order of paternity orders the change.

Adoption

When a legal adoption is complete, the investigating agency issues an adoption report (VS-44), which states that the adoption is final and lists all relevant information about the child and the adopting parent(s). The adoption report will include the child's birth name. If the child's name was changed as part of the adoption, the adoption order will state the child's new name. (This is usual but not legally required. For instance, in the case of a stepparent adoption, an older child may or may not take the stepparent's name.)

Following state law, the court clerk forwards the report and the adoption order to the State Registrar of Vital Statistics no later than five days after the adoption is finalized. (Cal. Health & Safety Code §§ 102625–102710.) If the child was born in California, the State Registrar will issue a new birth certificate for the child. This birth certificate will include the child's name as it is listed on the adoption order, the time and place of birth, and the names and ages of the adopting parents. No reference is made to the adoption. If the adopting parents wish, the new birth certificate will not list the name and address of the birth hospital or the color and race of the birth parents. (Cal. Health & Safety Code § 102645.)

Gender Correction

It's possible to have a new birth certificate issued when the original lists incorrect gender information. For example, if you name your daughter Billy and somehow the birth certificate lists her sex as male, you can get it changed. The purpose of this rule is to provide a remedy for people whose birth certificates are wrong due to an error by the birth hospital or local registrar. An application under this statute must include one of the following:

- an affidavit (a statement signed under penalty of perjury) from the administrator or representative of the birth hospital, acknowledging that the incorrect gender information is due to the hospital's error
- an affidavit from the local registrar, acknowledging that the incorrect gender information is due to the registrar's error, or
- an affidavit from the physician attending the birth of the applicant *and* an affidavit from the mother or father or a relative of the applicant who was at least five years old at the time of the applicant's birth, verifying that the applicant's gender was different at birth from that listed on the birth certificate. See the following examples of these types of affidavits.

A birth certificate issued under this statute will appear no different from an original birth certificate. (Cal. Health & Safety Code §§ 103446–103449.)

Affidavit of Steven Hart, Presiding Doctor at Birth of John Michael Mills

I am an obstetrician and have been licensed to practice in the State of California since 1991.

I presided at the birth of John Michael Mills to parents Mary Mills and Ted Mills at Beth Israel Hospital in Los Angeles, California, on March 10, 2007. Although John's birth certificate states that he is female, at the time John was born, he was male.

I declare under penalty of perjury under the laws of the State of California that the foregoing is true and correct.

Dated: ___[date]_____

___[Signature of Steven Hart]___
Steven Hart

Affidavit of Melissa Mills, Mother of John Michael Mills

I am the mother of John Michael and I was born on March 8, 1978. I gave birth to John Michael Mills on March 10, 2007.

Although John's birth certificate states that he is female, at the time John was born, he was male.

I declare under penalty of perjury under the laws of the State of California that the foregoing is true and correct.

Dated: ___[date]_____

___[Signature of Melissa Mills]___
Melissa Mills

This process cannot be used to change the gender listed on a birth certificate following a gender transition as an adult. See Chapter 7 for information on changing your name and gender designation.

Fixing Clerical Errors on Birth Certificates

Occasionally, errors are made on original birth certificates. Typically these are typographical errors—for example, a child's name is listed as "Nose" instead of "Rose." Sometimes an item is left blank, such as a child's first or middle name. You can correct a minor error like these by attaching an amendment to your birth certificate with the corrected information. Although the birth certificate itself is not changed, the correction becomes an official part of the record. (Cal. Health & Safety Code §§ 103225–103255.)

CAUTION

Birth certificate corrections only work for minor errors. The Office of Vital Records will not accept substantial name changes using a clerical error type amendment. An example of a substantial change is completely replacing a first name—for example, changing "Mary" to "Phyllis." Other substantial changes include gender errors and paternity errors. You are eligible to obtain a new birth certificate for these types of errors—rather than merely an amendment—but you will have to fulfill more specific and rigorous requirements. (See "Adding a Father's Name" for missing paternity information, "Changing a Father's Name" for incorrect paternity information, and "Gender Correction," above, for gender error.)

To accomplish an amendment of a clerical error, you must provide two affidavits—statements signed under penalty of perjury—in which the signers testify to the error. The affidavits must be completed by:

- you (either on your own behalf or on behalf of your child), and
- any other credible person with information about the error. A hospital official should complete an affidavit whenever possible. (See the sample affidavits, above, for guidance in creating affidavits for this situation.)

Depending on the circumstances, the correct form will be either Form VS-24, Application to Amend a Record, or Form VS-107, Application to Complete Name of Child by Supplemental Name Report— Birth. The Office of Vital Records supplies affidavit forms, as well. (See "Forms and Assistance From the OVR," below.)

TIP

Promptly fix birth certificate mistakes. There is no charge for correcting errors to a birth certificate if the change is made within one year of the child's birth. Also, you are more likely to have your proposed change approved if you act promptly.

Adding a Parent's New Name to a Child's Birth Certificate

After a parent completes a court ordered name change, an amendment showing the parent's new name can be added to the child's birth certificate. The attachment indicates that the parent is "AKA" (also known as) and gives the new name. Adding an attachment does not change the child's name, and it will not result in a new birth certificate being issued. Contact the OVR for information about how to do this.

Adults and Birth Certificates

Adults can amend their own birth certificates after a court-ordered name change. Most people don't bother, because amending a birth certificate doesn't have any legal affect on the acceptance of a new name, but it can be done. Adults are rarely able to have entirely new birth certificates issued, but the few circumstances where this is permitted are described below.

Adding New Name After Court-Ordered Name Change

If you were born in California and had your name changed in court, you can have an amendment attached to your birth certificate to reflect your new name. You can use this procedure after a name change by court petition, as well as after any other court order that changes your name, such as a divorce order or adoption. There is only one requirement: The court order changing your name must have been issued by a court in California or any other state or territory of the United States. (Cal. Health & Safety Code §§ 103400–103410.) The amendment does not actually change the content of the birth certificate itself, but it is physically attached to your birth certificate and becomes an official part of that record. The correct form for this situation is Form VS-23, Application for Amendment of Birth Record to Reflect Court Order Change of Name. (See "Forms and Assistance From the OVR," below.) A court order is required to amend your birth certificate.

Sex Change Operation (Court Order)

A person born in California who has undergone a surgical sex change operation may obtain a new birth certificate that changes the name and gender listed on the birth certificate. See Chapter 7 for more information.

Offensive Racial Description

While not a name change, an applicant can request a new birth certificate if the original contains a derogatory, demeaning, or colloquial racial description. To have the birth certificate changed, you must identify the term you want changed, provide an accurate racial description, and pay a specified fee. (Cal. Health & Safety Code §§ 103350–103375.)

EXAMPLE:

Sharlene Jones was born in 1951 to an African American father and a Caucasian mother. The attendant who filled out her birth certificate listed her race as "mulatto." Sharlene has always hated this term, but never realized there was anything she could do to change her birth certificate. When she learns that she does have recourse, she decides she wants to change her birth certificate and that she wants to be listed as an African American. She applies to the state and is issued a new birth certificate.

Gender Corrections and Minor Errors

Adults, like children, can have their birth certificates changed if the gender was listed incorrectly or a minor clerical error occurred. See above.

Forms and Assistance From the OVR

The proper application forms for any of the situations discussed in this section are available from the Office of Vital Records, Department of Public Health, 1501 Capital Avenue–MS.5103, Sacramento (street address) or Office of Vital Records, MS 5103, P.O. Box 997410, Sacramento, CA 95899-7410 (mailing address). Telephone is 916-445-2684.

Some of the forms you'll need are available online, but others are not. You can order forms at the DPH website, at www.cdph.ca.gov. You can also view an FAQ about amendments at www.cdph. ca.gov. Click the link for Birth, Death, and Marriage Certificates. Some forms are also available from local county recorders. If you have questions that are not answered by the FAQ, or if you do not have access to the Internet, you can call 916-445-2684. Don't expect to talk to someone right away; you will have to leave your name and phone number and wait for a call back. The website may be a faster way to order forms.

Basics of the Court Petition

There is no need to hire a lawyer in order to petition a court to change your name. A name change petition is a straightforward legal matter that nonlawyers can easily understand and accomplish. In fact, thousands of nonlawyers have successfully handled their own name changes (many with the help of this book). Courts are accustomed to seeing petitions filed by nonlawyers for name change matters.

You will be petitioning (asking) a court to officially change your name. As we describe in Chapter 1, this process is quite simple. You will:

- fill out a few straightforward forms (included on the CD-ROM in the back of this book and in the appendix, and available online)
- file the forms with your local superior court
- pay the filing fee (unless you are eligible for a fee waiver)
- arrange for a local newspaper to publish a notice of your proposed change, and
- possibly, but not necessarily, appear in person before the court.

It's also possible that you might need to serve (deliver) papers about the name change petition of a minor if the other parent doesn't agree or if you are a legal guardian. We also tell you how to do this, in Chapter 8.

It will take a bit of time and money to complete these steps. But when you are finished, your name will officially be changed. There will be no need to hassle with bureaucrats to get your new name accepted, because you'll have a court order backing up your new name. Given the movement toward more stringent requirements for having your name changed on personal documents, we think the time and expense you'll spend going to court will be worth it.

TIP

Those married or divorced in California have an easier option. For people divorced in California, a simple one-page form, Ex Parte Application for Restoration of Former Name After Entry of Judgment, can be filed in the divorce case, even years after the divorce was final. Therefore, if you were divorced in California and want to return to a birth or former name, you don't need to use the regular Court Petition method. (Instead, see "Divorce and Annulment," in Chapter 4.) Also, if you are changing your name because you got married, you can simply use your marriage certificate to have your official documents changed, without going through the court petition process.

This chapter will show you how to prepare a name change petition for yourself and for other family members, including a minor child. Here in this introductory section, we give you information about how to use this chapter, as well as a brief overview of special issues involved in changing a child's name. We also advise you how to access information from your local court about name changes.

Finally, we describe in detail the forms you'll need to file for a name change, and show you how to fill them out.

SKIP AHEAD

If you have had a sex change operation, you will need to fill out and file different forms. Skip ahead to Chapter 7, which deals specifically with the process and the forms for changing your name and the gender listed on your birth certificate.

In this chapter, we'll concentrate on the four basic name change forms—the ones everyone changing their name will need to file. Most people can do the job with just these basic forms. But in the following instances you also need to complete one or more additional forms:

- if you have a low income and want to apply for a waiver of court fees and costs (instructions are in Chapter 8), or
- if you are the legal guardian of a child and are applying to change the child's name (instructions are in "Forms for Legal Guardians," below).

After you have finished filling out the forms described in this chapter (or in Chapter 7, if you are petitioning for a change of name and gender), you'll go on to Chapter 8, which contains step-by-step instructions for filing your petition, arranging for the required publication, and serving the papers, if necessary, on a minor's relatives. Chapter 9 will explain how to find out whether you will need to attend a hearing, and how to prepare for it if you are required to attend.

Filing on Behalf of a Child

Petitioning a court to change a child's name is often as easy as filing a petition on your own behalf. You will fill out all the same forms and take all the same basic steps. However, the judge will approve the change only if it is in the child's best interest. If the other parent objects to your proposed name change, a contested hearing will be held and, depending on the facts of the situation, the chances of its being approved may drop substantially.

The "Best Interests of the Child" Standard

A court will change a child's name only when it is in the "best interests of the child." (Cal. Civ. Proc. Code § 1278.5.) Unfortunately, because the test is applied on a case-by-case basis, this rather vague standard can leave plenty of wiggle room for reasonable people's opinions to differ. Some situations are more straightforward than others, however.

Situations in Which the Court Is Likely to Grant a Child's Petition

Here are three common situations in which a court is likely to approve a petition to change a child's name:

- Both parents petition together (whether they are married or not).
- One parent petitions and, after notification, the other doesn't object.
- One parent petitions and the second parent can't be found or has abandoned the child.

Where both of a child's parents petition the court together to change their child's name, a court is highly likely to grant the name change. This is true whether or not the parents are currently a couple.

EXAMPLE:

Leila Norris and James Gold were living together but not married when they had their daughter Jasmine Norris-Gold. Now, three years later, they are ready to get married. They have decided they want to go by a new family name, Trey, in honor of Leila's grandfather. They petition the court to change all three of their last names to Trey.

EXAMPLE:

Ted and Jessica Hie were divorced when their son William was three. Jessica and Ted have shared joint custody of William, even after Jessica remarried and became Jessica Yates. Recently, Ted decided that he is going to move to the East Coast. Both Ted and Jessica agree that since William will now be spending nearly all of his time with Jessica, her second husband, and their new baby, Jasper Yates, William should share their last name. Ted and Jessica petition the court to change their son's name to William Yates.

In both of these examples, the child's parents are in agreement and are petitioning the court together to change their child's name. Because both parents are present and in agreement, a court would be very likely to grant these name changes. This is true despite the fact that in the second example the parents are divorced and the child's name will no longer match his birth father's name.

Another common situation where children's name changes are routinely approved involves parental abandonment. This most commonly happens when a father fails to visit or support a child for an extended period. (See Chapter 8 for information on notifying a parent who has abandoned the child.)

EXAMPLE:

Jerri and Ben Best got a divorce after five years of marriage. Their daughter, Becky, was three at the time. Jerri returned to her birth name, Jerri Moran, and she was given full custody of Becky. Ben paid child support for one year, but after that, his checks stopped coming and he disappeared. After two years without contact or support from Ben, Jerri applied to a court for an order that she did not have to serve Ben personally with notice of the petition, and to change Becky's surname to Moran. The judge approved the change, finding that it was in Becky's best interests to do so.

Another common situation in which name changes are routinely approved involves a petition by one parent and no opposition from the other. With only the parent who wants to make the change appearing in court, the judge is likely to approve it as long as the petitioning parent can show that the other parent has been officially notified of the proposed change and has failed to appear.

EXAMPLE:

Using the same example, this time assume that Ben kept paying his child support and occasionally visited Becky. But after a few years, because Jerri has full custody of Becky, she thinks Becky should have her surname. She contacts Ben and he says he's fine with it—but he doesn't want to deal with the court so he won't sign any papers. Although Ben is still involved in Becky's life, if he does not actively oppose the petition, the court will probably still find it is in Becky's best interest to be Becky Moran.

Situations in Which the Court May Not Grant the Petition

When both parents have maintained relationships with the child and one opposes the name change, courts are usually reluctant to grant it, and will never do so without a hearing. This doesn't mean a court won't ultimately approve the change—it just means the court will listen to each parent's argument and decide what is in the child's best interests. In making its determination, the court will consider:

- the length of time the child has used the current last name
- the effect of the name change on the preservation of the relationship with both parents
- the status and strength of the child's relationship with each parent
- the need of the child to identify with a new family unit through use of a common name
- for older children, the wishes of the child, and
- any other facts the court finds important in a given case.

The court will balance these factors to help it decide which name is in the child's best interest. Consider the following example.

EXAMPLE:

Carol and Tom Tuschman were married in March and separated by May—together just long enough to get pregnant. Their baby, Liz, was born three weeks after their divorce was final. In mediation, they agreed to 50-50 joint custody. Carol returned to her birth name, Chen. She has been married twice before, and each time returned to Chen. Now, she wants Liz to be a Chen, like her two young boys from previous marriages. Tom wants Liz to stay a

Tuschman, like his two teenage boys. Tom says that, given Carol's marriage record, she'll just want to change the baby's name the next time she marries. He also thinks that Liz should bear his name. Carol says she's willing to let Liz have a hyphenated name combining Chen and Tuschman, but because Liz primarily lives in a Chen household, it's silly for her to be called Tuschman.

This example is based on the case of *Douglass v. Douglass*, 205 Cal. App. 3d 1046 (1988). In that case, the court agreed with the mother—reasoning that because the mother would probably be the primary caretaker, the baby should go by her name. The court ordered the baby's birth certificate to bear a hyphenated combination of the names but that the baby should go by the mother's name only. If the case were to happen today, the court might rule differently. Hyphenated names are much more common now, and a current court might approve one for all purposes and not agree with the expert witness who testified in the Douglass case that hyphenated names are "too much to saddle a child with."

EXAMPLE:

Joe and Jane Evans divorced when their son, Brian, was two. Jane, who kept her married name, was given full custody of Brian, and Joe was ordered to pay child support. Jane stopped receiving checks six months after the divorce, no matter

how often she called Joe to remind him. A year later, she couldn't even find Joe. Jane got remarried to Bill Sears and became Jane Sears. Brian, now four, thinks of Bill as his dad and of Bill's two sons as his brothers. Jane petitioned to have Brian's last name changed from Evans to Sears. She hired a process server, who tracked down Joe and served him with the papers. Joe then filed an objection with the court.

Courts will always pause and look at the facts when one parent objects to a name change. On these facts, though, a court will likely be willing to change Brian's name despite Joe's objections. Joe has been out of the picture, by his own choosing, for almost half of Brian's young life. He cannot point to a strong father-child relationship. Furthermore, the mother-child relationship is strong, and Brian feels close with his new family. But the court's result might be different in the following situation.

EXAMPLE:

Imagine that Jane and Joe divorced when Brian was ten. Joe slid out of the picture when Brian was twelve, and Jane married Bill Sears when Brian was 14. Jane and Bill immediately had a child, so when Brian is 15 he has a new sister named Jill Sears. Jane asks Brian if he wants his name to be Sears instead of Evans, and knowing how she feels about his father, he says yes. Jane petitions the court to change Brian's name to Sears. Again, Joe files an objection in court.

In this situation, Brian has gone by the name Brian Evans for 15 years. His father was in his life for 12 years. So, as compared to the previous example, Brian would likely feel much more attached to the name Evans, and he probably will always think of Joe as his father and Bill as his stepfather, even though Joe hasn't contacted him in three years. Because Brian is a teenager, he probably has an opinion about the name change—an opinion that may or may not be the same as what he told his mother. A judge would likely interview Brian and see how he feels. Brian's response may be the main factor in the court's decision.

Notifying Interested Parties— Service of Process

Although it isn't always possible to guess how a court will decide a child's name change controversy, one thing is certain— both living parents have the right to know about their child's proposed name change. If you are the child's parent and are filing a petition alone without the child's other parent, the court will require you to notify the other parent. You must do this even if you have sole custody of your child. Similarly, if you are the child's legal guardian, you will need to provide notice to the child's parents or, if the child's

parents are unknown or no longer alive, to the child's living grandparents.

This official notification is called "service of process." You "serve" the nonfiling parent by giving the parent a copy of a legal form called Order to Show Cause. In certain circumstances, a court will waive the service of process requirement. If the father has abandoned his child and the mother cannot locate him, or if the father has a history of abuse, the court may not require you to serve him. (See Chapter 8 for much more on this subject.)

Getting Information From Your Superior Court

The superior court for your county is where you'll file your name change petition. If you don't know the location of your county courthouse, you can look it up in the government section of your phone book or find it online. Some of the larger counties have a large main courthouse in the biggest city and several branch courts in small cities. For example, Los Angeles County has many superior court branches. If there is a branch court close to you, it usually makes sense to file your papers there.

Before you get started, you'll need additional information on filing a name change petition with your local court. You can find the phone number of the court in the government pages of the phone book or at the court's website. To find the website for your local court, go to the California Judicial Council website at www.courtinfo.ca.gov/court/find.htm. Click on the link to your local superior court.

The information you need might be available on the court's website. If you don't find it there, call the clerk to ask the following questions:

- the proper branch of the court for filing your papers (tell the clerk which city or town you live in)
- the mailing address of the court
- the street address of the court—if it is different from the mailing address
- the filing fee for a name change petition (if you cannot afford the fees, you may be able to have them waived; see Chapter 8)
- whether you need to file any local forms (particular to your local court) along with the state's standardized name change forms contained in this book and, if needed, the best way to get them (specifically, ask whether you need to file a Civil Case Cover Sheet Addendum, a form that helps the courts easily see what type of case you are filing), and
- whether there are local court rules for name changes (some courts have very specific requirements for form preparation, service of process, and attendance at hearings, in addition to the statewide rules set out in this book).

Again, some of this information may be available on the court's website, which you can access as described above.

Getting Your Papers in Order

The forms required for a name change are easier to complete than most job applications. We can't say that filling out the forms will be fun, but it can be satisfying to do something on your own that you would otherwise pay a lawyer hundreds of dollars to do for you.

The four basic forms for a Name Change Petition are:

- **Petition for Change of Name ("Petition").** This form—plus its attachment called **Name and Information About the Person Whose Name Is to Be Changed**—is your official request to have your name changed and provides the necessary background information to process your request.
- **Order to Show Cause for Change of Name ("Order to Show Cause").** This is used by the court to order anyone who might want to contest your name change to come forward.
- **Decree Changing Name ("Decree").** This form, when signed by a judge, will officially change your name. It is also commonly referred to as a court order.
- **Civil Case Cover Sheet ("Cover Sheet").** This is a simple form that goes on top of the packet of forms you'll be filing. It quickly tells the court what type of case you're filing.

CD-ROM

The CD-ROM contains blank versions of these four forms. You can also find them at the California Judicial Council website, www.courtinfo.ca.gov/forms, or at your local superior court. The forms can even be filled out online, as described below.

All these forms are produced by the state for use in every county. This book contains copies of these forms, current as of when this book went to press.

Tips on Completing Forms

Most forms follow a standard fill-in-the-blanks format. Before you begin, here is some basic information you'll need to know about completing forms:

- You'll find blank versions of all the required forms set out in this chapter on the CD-ROM at the back of this book. As we've noted above, the forms are also available on the Judicial Council website at www.courtinfo.ca.gov/forms. The forms can be filled out online and printed from your computer. It's a good idea to print out a blank copy of the form, work on filling it in by hand until you're sure it's right, and then use it as a cheat sheet to fill out the form on the computer. That way you're less likely to make a mistake.

Be Sure to Use Current Forms

The forms in this book were current when it went to press, in September 2010. If you plan on filing your forms on or after January 1, 2011, you'll need to make sure that the forms have not been revised (the Judicial Council often tinkers with its forms, and issues revised forms on January 1 and July 1). Here's how to check for revisions and get the new forms, if needed.

Go to the Council's website at www.courtinfo.ca.gov/forms. Choose the "Name Changes" group of forms and scroll through the list for the form you are interested in. Check the "Date Revised"—if the date is after January 1, 2011, print out and use the new form (or complete the form online and print it). Unless the forms have been seriously overhauled, the information in this chapter will still help you with the new forms—but watch for inconsistencies.

- All forms should be completed carefully and neatly, preferably using a computer or typewriter. It is best to use the larger type size. Some courts may refuse to accept forms with smaller type. If you do not have access to a typewriter, the court may provide one for public use, or a local library may rent them. You can also check the yellow pages for typing and document preparation services; these are small companies that prepare forms for nonlawyers at

Terms Used in Name Change Forms

To complete the court forms required for a name change, you'll need to know these essential terms. They are used throughout the instructions.

Present Name. The complete name that will be changed. Even if you (or the child you're petitioning for) have already been using what will be your new official name, fill in your old name when you are asked for your "present" name. If you have used a number of names over the years, read Chapter 2 to help determine which name to use when asked for your official present name. List any other names you have formerly gone by after your official present name as AKAs (also known as). For example, Joanna Barkley, AKA (or a.k.a.) Joanna Stern.

Proposed Name. The complete new name by which you want to be known. Even if you are already using this name for many purposes, it's still your proposed name.

Person Whose Name Is to Be Changed. This is the person whose name will change. Use the present name here—not the proposed name. If the person has gone by a number of names (see "Present Name," above), list the present name, followed by other names as AKAs. There may be more than one Person Whose Name Is to Be Changed per Petition—for example, a mother and a child may both be seeking name changes. For a minor (person under age 18), list the minor's name and the words "a minor" (for example, "Kevin Apple, a minor")

Petitioner. The person(s) completing the forms and requesting the name change. Although the Petitioner and the Person Whose Name Is to Be Changed are often the same, they can be different people when, for example, an adult seeks a name change for a minor. There also may be more than one Petitioner, if, for instance, a couple is petitioning together to change their child's name. Every place a form requires you to write the name of the Petitioner, write the names of all the Petitioners.

---

a reasonable cost. (See Chapter 11 for more about finding additional help.)

- Your court will probably accept handwritten forms if you print clearly and neatly, preferably in black ink. If you want to submit handwritten forms, call the filing clerk beforehand to make sure they'll be accepted.

How to Complete the Caption

At the top of the first page of each form, you'll find several boxes with blank spaces, which together are referred to as the "caption." The caption will be identical on all your name change forms, meaning you will fill it in the same way on each. Here's how.

Attorney or Party Without Attorney. Fill in your present name in capital letters, followed by your mailing address and telephone number. You may also list your fax number and email address if you wish. (The court will not contact you via email, so if you don't want your email address to appear in the public court record, just leave that space blank.) After "Attorney For," write "In Pro Per" (this means you are representing yourself).

Superior Court of California, County of. In capital letters after the words "County of," fill in the county in which you are filing your papers. In the spaces provided underneath, fill in the court's street address, mailing address, city, and zip code. Also fill in the branch name, if there is one.

Petition of (Name of each petitioner). Again, fill in your own present name in all capital letters. Do this even if you are petitioning to change your child's name— you are still the Petitioner. Include the names of any other petitioners here, too. If another person (typically the other parent in a child's name change) will be signing and filing the forms with you, that person is a petitioner as well.

Petition for Change of Name. This is the title of this particular form. Each form has a title, such as "Petition for Change of Name" or "Order to Show Cause for Change of Name." Leave the title as it is.

Case Number. This is where the court clerk will write or stamp your case number when you file your papers. Leave this space blank for now, because you don't have a case number yet. When you file your Petition, the clerk will open a file for you and assign you a case number. If you later need to file additional papers as part of this same name change petition, you'll need to use this number. Carefully copy the case number from the papers you already filed onto any papers you file later.

Basic Name Change Forms

This section will walk you through the basic forms, line by line.

Petition for Change of Name

The Petition for Change of Name is your official request to the court to change your name and/or the name(s) of other person(s). This form, along with its attachment, "Name and Information of Person Whose Name Is to Be Changed," will provide the court with the facts it needs to consider your request. You can use a single Petition to change more than one person's name—such as a couple or parent and children. However, you need to fill out a separate "Name and Information" sheet for each person whose name you want to change.

Petition for Change of Name— First Page

Here are the instructions for filling out the Petition for Change of Name.

CD-ROM

You'll find a blank copy of the Petition for Change of Name on the CD-ROM. You can also download the form at www.courtinfo.ca.gov/forms.

Caption. Follow the instructions in "How to Complete the Caption," above.

Item 1. Fill in your present name here, as the Petitioner. Do not fill in your proposed name, even if you are already using it. Write your full, complete present name. Do not use nicknames or initials (unless your full name actually contains an initial that does not stand for anything). Put in the name(s) of any other Petitioners as well.

Item 2. Fill in the present name and the proposed name of each person whose name will be changed. As discussed in Chapter 2, if the person has used more than one name, list that person's current official name followed by AKAs. Use a separate line for each person, starting with (a) and working your way down. In the first blank on each line, list one person's present name, and in the second blank of that line, list the same person's proposed name. If you are seeking to change the name of more than four persons, check the box at the end of Item 2 and type up the remaining names on an attachment form.

CAUTION

Filing jointly may cause problems in rare circumstances. It's not likely, but it is possible that the court clerk might object to

you using this form to change the name of more than one adult. (You won't have any problem if the additional people listed are minors.) Even though the form clearly provides for the possibility that more than one adult would petition together, some clerks insist that each adult must have a separate petition. If this happens, ask to speak to a supervisor and find out what basis the clerk has for trying to require separate petitions. If the clerk tells you the law requires it, make sure you get the specific code section the clerk is relying on. You might want to contact a lawyer for help if you can't persuade the clerk to file a single petition. (Just remember that it might be more cost effective to simply pay the second filing fee than to pay for a lawyer's help.)

CD-ROM

There is a Judicial Council form called "Attachment" that you can use for creating an attachment. A copy is included on the CD-ROM, or you can download a copy at www.courtinfo.ca.gov/forms/fillable/mc025.pdf.

The attachment should look like this:

"Attachment 2—Continuation of Item 2"

	Present Name		Proposed Name
(e)	John Meyers	changed to	John Dietz
(f)	Julie Meyers	changed to	Julie Dietz

CAUTION

Domestic violence alert. If you are a participant in the state's address confidentiality program for victims of domestic violence and stalking and you are changing your name to avoid these problems, you do not need to list your proposed new name on your forms. In each place where a form asks you to list your proposed name, you can instead state, "confidential and on file with the Secretary of State pursuant to the provisions of the address confidentiality program." (See Cal. Civ. Proc. Code §§ 1277(b), 1278(b).)

Item 3. This line states that you are asking the court to order all persons who might want to object to your proposed name change(s) to come forward. You don't need to do anything to this item.

Item 4. At the end of this line, write the number of persons whose name you want changed who are minors (not yet 18 years old).

Item 5. This Item asks for information on the Petitioner, if the Petition is filed on behalf of a child or children. If you are not changing any minors' names, skip this Item. But if you are petitioning on behalf of a minor, mark the box that best describes your relationship and the relationship of any other Petitioner to the child. If your relationship is not described by choices (a)–(e), mark (f) and use the space provided to type a brief description of your relationship (for example, "relative").

Item 6(a). This Item tells the court how many "Name and Information" sheets you will be attaching to this Petition. Because you need to attach a separate "Name and Information" sheet for each person whose name will be changed, this number should be the same as the number of lines you filled in at Item 2.

Items 6(b)–(f). This line refers to items on the "Name and Information" sheet, as a way of showing that they are really a part of this form. You don't need to enter anything on this line.

Petition for Change of Name— Name and Information Sheet(s)

Here are the instructions for filling out the Name and Information attachment to the Petition. Complete a separate Name and Information attachment for every person whose name you are changing.

CD-ROM

You'll find a blank copy of the Name and Information Sheet on the CD-ROM at the back of the book. You can also download the form at www.courtinfo.ca.gov/fillable/nc110.pdf.

Caption. Fill in your present name in the box labeled "Petition Of." Leave the Case Number box blank; as noted above, the court clerk will put your newly assigned case number here when you file your papers. At the upper right-hand corner, below the box for the case number, enter the required numbers to describe how many pages you are filing and which page this is. For example, if you are seeking to change only your own name, type in "Attachment 1 of 1." If you are seeking to change your own name and that of your child, you will have two attachments and on the first attachment, this item should read "Attachment 1 of 2"; on the second it will read "Attachment 2 of 2."

Item 6(b). Check the "self" box if you are filling out this attachment in order to change your own name. Check the "other" box if you are filling it out on behalf of someone else.

Item (1). Fill in the present name of the Person Whose Name Is to Be Changed (we'll call that person "Person" for the rest of this form). As described above, if the Person goes by a number of names, list the present name followed by the other names as AKAs.

Item (2). Fill in the proposed new name of the Person.

Item (3). Fill in the Person's birth date and check the appropriate box to mark whether the Person is younger than 18 or is 18 or older.

Item (4). Fill in the Person's city and state of birth—including the country if the Person was born outside of the United States (you need not be a citizen to have your name changed).

Item (5). Check the correct box for the Person's sex.

Item (6). Fill in the Person's complete current home address, including county.

This must be the same county where you will be filing the name change papers. There is no time requirement for residency—the Person may have lived in the county for one week or 20 years.

Item 6(c). Briefly state why you are seeking a name change (or why the Person is seeking a name change). Because state law holds that every adult has the right to change his or her name, the court should grant your Petition unless you are seeking it for one of the prohibited reasons discussed in Chapter 3. Just state your reason as simply as possible. In the following sidebars, we list examples of language you may be able to use. To make it easier to locate what you need, we have arranged the examples under children and adults.

Item 6(d). Check the box that describes your relationship to the Person. If you are filing your Petition on behalf of yourself and another person, your response to this item will obviously be different on the Name and Information sheet you fill out for yourself and those you fill out on behalf of the others.

Item 6(e). If you are filling out an attachment on behalf of a person younger than 18, use this section to fill in the name and home address of the child's father and mother. If, as is likely, you are one of the child's parents, fill in your name on the appropriate line and write "(Petitioner)" after it. If one of the parents is dead, put the word "(deceased)" after the name. If you do not know who one of the parents

Reasons for an Adult's Name Change

You may want to use or adapt the explanations below when you complete Item 6(c) of your Petition, explaining to the court why you want to change your name (see the next sidebar for examples of reasons for a child's name change). Change the language of any of the examples to better suit you. If you have already been using the proposed name, you have a great reason for the name change request, because one of the purposes of the court petition method is to make an official record of usage name changes. If that is your situation, include the words "is already known by" in your explanation.

- Petitioner's present name is inconvenient, hard to spell, unappealing, embarrassing, and confusing [use words that apply].
- Petitioner's proposed name is convenient and [he/she] wishes to be known by this name in all [his/her] personal and business affairs.
- Petitioner's proposed name better suits [his/her] present identity. Therefore Petitioner [is already known by and] wishes to be known by [his/her] proposed name in all [his/her] social and business affairs.

- Petitioner's proposed name is an ancestral name. Petitioner [is already known by and] wishes to be known by this name in all [his/her] social and business affairs.
- Petitioner is already known by [his/her] proposed name in [his/her] profession, and wishes to be known by [his/her] professional name in all [his/her] social as well as professional affairs. [For couples] Because Petitioners are husband and wife, they wish to be known by the same last name.
- Petitioner's proposed name is her birth [or former] name. Petitioner feels her proposed name better suits her present identity and therefore she [is already known by and] wishes to be known by her proposed name in all her social and business affairs.
- [For a couple changing each partner's last name to a combination of the two names] Petitioners want to share the same last name, and their proposed surname is a combination of their two family names.

is, fill in "unknown." If you do not know the address of one of the parents, write "address unknown." (Chapter 8 tells you what to do if you don't know where the other parent is.)

If you are a child's legal guardian and both of the child's parents are dead, use

the space after (3) to fill in the names, relationships, and home addresses of known close relatives such as sisters, brothers, aunts, uncles, and grandparents. If no close relatives are known, type in the words, "As far as known to Petitioner, [Minor] has no near relatives."

Reasons for Children's Name Changes

If you are petitioning on behalf of a child, remember that the court will grant the name change if it is in "the best interests of the child." In Item 6(c), briefly tell the court why you believe the child will be better off with a name change. Although you cannot officially change a child's name by the usage method, be sure to mention it if the child is already known by the proposed name.

- Petitioner was awarded custody of [Minor] upon her divorce on [date]. [Minor]'s natural father has failed to [regularly] make child support payments. No payments have been received since [date of last payment]. [Minor]'s father does not show parental interest in the child and has not [regularly] exercised his visitation rights since [date of last visit]. Petitioner has changed her surname [by remarriage or by returning to her birth or former name]. It is in [Minor]'s best interests, preventing inconvenience, to have the same surname as [his/her] mother [and stepfather, half-brother, and so on].

- [Minor's parents have both died/Minor's mother has passed away and Minor's father is unknown.] [Minor] has been living in the household of Petitioner since [date]. Petitioner is [Minor]'s [specify relationship, such as legal guardian, relative, or adult friend]. It is in the best interests of [Minor] to have the same surname as the Petitioner, preventing inconvenience.

- [Minor] is mature enough to choose [his/her] own name, and wishes to be known by [his/her] proposed name. Petitioner consents to this change of name and also prefers the proposed name.

- Petitioner was awarded custody of [Minor] upon her divorce on [date]. Petitioner has changed her surname [by remarriage or by returning to her birth or former name]. It is in [Minor]'s best interests, preventing inconvenience, to have the same surname as [his/her] mother [and stepfather, half-brother, and so on]. [Minor's natural father consents to the proposed name change.]

Item 6(f). Every adult seeking a name change must fill out and sign this declaration to state whether or not that person is in state prison or on parole and whether or not he or she is a convicted sex offender. Check the boxes that apply to you and sign the statement. If you are in state prison, on parole, or a convicted sex offender, see the sidebar below for more information on filing your Petition.

Date and Signature. Generally, you (and any other Petitioner) must sign and date the Petition on the last attached page.

However, if this "Name and Information" sheet is not the last attachment to your petition, you need not sign it. Instead, check the box to the right side of the page, below the signature lines, that states "Signature of Petitioners Follows Last Attachment."

Petitioning If You Are in Prison, on Parole, or a Sex Offender

If you are in state prison, the court will not hear your Petition unless you have the written approval of the Director of Corrections. The decision whether to grant you permission is entirely at the discretion of the Director. (See Cal. Civ. Proc. Code § 1279.5(b).)

If you are on parole, the court will not hear your Petition without the written approval of your parole agent or probation officer. By state law, your parole agent or probation officer must determine whether your name change would pose a security risk to the community. (See Cal. Civ. Proc. Code § 1279.5(c).)

If you are a registered sex offender (under Cal. Penal Code § 290), the court will change your name only if the court determines that granting your Petition "is in the best interest of justice" and will not adversely affect public safety. If the court grants your name change you must notify local authorities of the change within five days. (See Cal. Civ. Proc. Code § 1279.5(d).)

If this Name and Information sheet is the last attachment, date, print, or type your present name and sign in the spaces provided. If there is a second Petitioner, that person should do the same on the second line provided. Signing the document "under penalty of perjury" has the same effect as a sworn statement or oath, meaning you could be prosecuted under California law if you lie.

The page has space for only two Petitioners to sign. If you are filing with more than one other Petitioner, check the box at the left of the page, below the second signature line, that states "Add Additional Signature Lines for Additional Petitioners." On a separate sheet of paper, the additional Petitioners must print or type their names, and then sign and date the page. Accomplish this by following the same signature format you see on the printed form.

 CAUTION

Complete a Name and Information sheet for each person whose name will change. If you are petitioning for name changes for more than one person, make sure you complete a separate Name and Information sheet for each one. Staple all attachments to the back of the Petition.

Order to Show Cause for Change of Name

This form is the official court document by which the court notifies interested parties of your application and orders anyone who may oppose your proposed name change to come forward and voice their objection. In theory at least, the public will be aware of this order because you will publish it in the legal notices section of a local newspaper once a week for four weeks.

However, it is extremely rare for anyone to object to an adult's name change petition.

You'll have to skip forward here just briefly to review the instructions for selecting a newspaper for publication, which are contained in Chapter 8. Once you have figured out what paper to use, you're ready to complete the Order to Show Cause for Change of Name. Following are the instructions for filling out this form.

CD-ROM

You'll find a blank copy of the Order to Show Cause for Change of Name on the CD-ROM at the back of the book. You can also download the form at www.courtinfo.ca.gov/forms.

Caption. Follow the instructions in "How to Complete the Caption," above.

Item 1. Fill in your present name and the name of any other Petitioner in the space on the first line.

Items 1(a)–(e). Fill in the present name and the proposed name of each person whose name will be changed. Use a separate line for each person, starting with (a) and working your way down. In the first blank on each line, list one person's present name, and in the second blank of that line, list the same person's proposed name. If you are seeking to change the name of more than five persons, check the box at the end of Item 1 and create an attachment form as described in "Basic Name Change Forms," above.

CAUTION

Domestic violence alert. If you are a participant in the state's address confidentiality program for victims of domestic violence and stalking and you are changing your name to avoid these problems, you do not need to list your proposed new name.

Item 2. This line states that the court is ordering all persons who might want to object to your proposed name change(s) to appear at the court and voice their concerns. You don't need to do anything with this item.

Item 2(a). Under the title, "Notice of Hearing," the clerk will fill in the date and time of the hearing and the department or room number in which it will be held. Do not fill in the information requested in the box yourself. The clerk will complete this item when you file your documents with the court.

Item 2(b). In the space provided, fill in the court's complete street address, unless it is the same as noted in the caption above, in which case you should check the appropriate box.

Item 3. In this item, specify how you will publicize this order. If your county has at least one newspaper of general circulation that has been certified to publish legal notices, mark the box at (a). Write the complete name of the newspaper you have selected in the space provided. See Chapter 8 for information on selecting a newspaper. If your county does not have a paper that is certified to publish legal notices, check the box at (b) and ask the court clerk how to complete the following blank. See "Getting Information From Your Superior Court," above, for information on contacting your court clerk.

Date and Judge's Signature. The judge will sign and date the Order here. Leave these items blank.

Decree Changing Name

The Decree Changing Name will be your official proof of your name change. Following are the instructions for filling out the Decree Changing Name.

CD-ROM

You'll find a blank copy of the Decree Changing Name on the CD-ROM at the back of the book. You can also download the form at www.courtinfo.ca.gov/fillable/nc130.pdf.

Caption. Follow the instructions in "How to Complete the Caption," above.

Item 1. Leave this item blank. The court clerk or judge will complete it.

Items 2(a)–(f). Leave these items blank— the judge will fill in the appropriate information.

Items 3(a)–(e). On these lines, fill in the present name and the proposed name of each person whose name will be changed. Use a separate line for each person, starting with (a) and working your way down. In the first blank on each line, list one person's present name, and in the second blank of that line, list the

same person's proposed name. If you are seeking to change the name of more than five persons, check the box at the end of Item 3 and create an attachment as described in "Basic Name Change Forms," above.

CAUTION

Domestic violence alert. If you are a participant in the state's address confidentiality program for victims of domestic violence and stalking and you are changing your name to avoid these problems, you do not need to list your proposed new name.

Date and Judge's Signature. The judge will sign and date the Decree here. Leave these items blank.

Civil Case Cover Sheet

All courts will require you to file a form called the "Civil Case Cover Sheet" with the rest of your documents. This form simply lists the fact that you are petitioning to change your name so the clerk can easily see what your case is about. File this form with the court at the same time as your Petition for Change of Name.

CD-ROM

We have filled out much of this form for you, and have provided it on the CD-ROM in the back of the book. We did this because the form should be filled out the same way in all name change petitions, except of course for the caption information personal to you. If you want to start with a blank form, you can download the form at www.courtinfo.ca.gov/fillable/cm010.pdf.

If you use the form we have provided, you need only fill in the following additional information.

Caption. Follow the directions in "How to Complete the Caption," above. Fill in your personal information, the court information, and the Case Name as you have done on every form.

Date and Signature. At the bottom of the page, fill in the date and your present name, then sign the form.

You have now completed all of the standard forms that you need to get your name change petition filed.

SKIP AHEAD

For legal guardians only. If you are not petitioning to change the name of a child who is your ward, skip the next section and go on to Chapter 8 to learn how to file your documents and proceed with the name change.

Forms for Legal Guardians

The basic forms that we describe above will cover the needs of most name change applicants. If you are a legal guardian of a child and are applying to change the child's name, you will need to file two additional forms.

First, the court will want information about the child's living relatives. You will need to file a form called a "Supplemental Attachment to Petition for Change of Name (Declaration of Guardian)," which tells the court about the child's family, your relationship to the child, and your reasons for changing the child's name. Second, you must also fill out a "Decree Changing Name (Change of Name of Minor by Guardian)" and file both, along with the Petition, Name and Information attachment, Order to Show Cause, and Civil Cover Sheet, described above. Instructions for these forms follow.

Declaration of Guardian

The Declaration of Guardian form (really a second attachment, along with the Name and Information attachment, to the Petition for Change of Name) explains to the court your relationship with the child and the child's relationship with his or her parents. You will also use it to tell the court why the change is in the best interests of the child and to supply other information, including the names of the child's grandparents (if you are a grandparent, you will list your own name). You must fill out a separate Declaration of Guardian for each child whose name you want to change, and attach them to the Petition. Following are directions for filling out the Declaration of Guardian.

CD-ROM

You'll find a blank copy of the Declaration of Guardian on the CD-ROM at the back of the book. You can also download the form at www.courtinfo.ca.gov/fillable/nc110g.pdf.

Caption. Because this form is an attachment to the Petition, it does not have its own full caption. In this abbreviated caption, you just need to write your name in the left-hand box.

Item 7a. Write your full name.

Item 7b. Write your complete current address.

Item 7c. In sections (1) and (2), write the name and address of the child for whom you are petitioning.

Item 7d. Use this item to tell the court the exact proceeding in which you were appointed the child's guardian. In the spaces provided, write (1) the county of the court that appointed you, (2) whether the department was Juvenile or Probate, (3) the guardianship case number, and (4) the date the appointment became final.

Item 7e. In lines (1) through (4), write the names and addresses of the child's four grandparents, if you know them. For those you don't know, write "unknown" in the name portion. For those that have died, write "(deceased)" after the name. If you don't know how to reach any of them, write "unknown" in the address portion. If you are one of the grandparents, list your own name.

Item 7f. In the space provided in Item 7f, explain why you are likely to remain the guardian of the child until the child becomes an adult. If you need extra space, check the box and continue your explanation on a separate page. There is a copy of a Judicial Council form called Attachment on the CD-ROM; you can also download the form at www.courtinfo.ca.gov/fillable/mc025.pdf. You can use this form as "Attachment 7f." (For help in completing Items 7f, 7g, and 7h, see "Sample Answers for Legal Guardians," below.)

Item 7g. Use this space to explain why it is unlikely that the child's parents will regain custody of the child. If you need extra space, check the box and continue your explanation on a separate page. Use the attachment form again and title that page "Attachment 7g."

Item 7h. In this space, tell the court why the change is in the child's best interest. You can also use this space to list any other relevant information about your guardianship or the proposed name change that you feel the court should know. If you need extra space, check the box and continue your explanation on a separate page, using the attachment form included in the appendix. Title that page "Attachment 7h."

Sample Answers for Legal Guardians

Here are some examples for answers to 7f, 7g, and 7h, which you can use to help you formulate your responses.

EXAMPLE 1:

7f: I am likely to maintain custody of Ann because I am her grandmother and she has lived with me since she was born.

7g: Ann's parents are unlikely to regain custody of her, because her mother, my daughter, died of a drug overdose, and her father is in prison. He will not come up for parole for another five years.

7h: It is in Ann's best interests to bear my family name because it is her mother's name also, and it will help her feel like she belongs in my nuclear family.

EXAMPLE 2:

7f: We are likely to maintain custody of Matthew because we are his godparents, and we have acted as parents to him since his parents, our close friends, were killed in a car accident.

7g: Matthew's parents will not regain custody of him because they are deceased.

7h: It is in Matthew's best interests to bear our family name because it will complete his transition into his new family.

Date and Signature. Write the date and your full name, and sign the signature line.

Guardian of. Underneath the signature line, write the child's complete current name.

Decree Changing Name of Minor (by Guardian)

Instead of filing a basic Decree Changing Name, as described above, a guardian must file a Decree Changing Name (Change of Name of Minor by Guardian). Like the basic Decree Changing Name, the Decree Changing Name (Change of Name of Minor by Guardian) is the document that the judge will use to change the child's name officially. When the court approves the name change, the judge will complete and sign this form. At that point, the child's name change is final. Your copy of this Decree will be your official proof of the child's name change.

You must file a separate Decree Changing Name (Change of Name of Minor by Guardian) for each child whose name you are changing. Following are the instructions for filling out this form.

CD-ROM

You'll find a blank copy of the Decree Changing Name (Change of Name of Minor by Guardian) on the CD-ROM at the back of the book. You can also download the form at www.courtinfo.ca.gov/fillable/nc130.pdf.

Caption. Follow the instructions in "How to Complete the Caption," above.

Item 1. Leave this sentence blank—the court clerk will fill in the date and courtroom (often called "department") of the hearing when you file your papers.

Items 2(a)–(j). Leave these items blank—the judge will fill in the appropriate information.

Item 3. On these lines, fill in the present name and the proposed name of the child whose name will be changed.

Date and Judge's Signature. The judge will sign and date the Decree here. Leave these items blank. Do not sign or date this form.

Legal guardians must also notify the child's family. Besides filing these two special forms, you will need to notify the child's family of the proposed name change. You must serve the Order to Show Cause on the child's parents or, if the child's parents are deceased or unknown, on the child's grandparents. See Chapter 8 for more about how to do this. ●

Changing Your Gender

The law has been slow to recognize the existence, let alone the legal needs, of transgender people. This state of affairs appears to be changing somewhat in California, although in small increments. In 2003, the California Judicial Council created special forms for legally changing your official gender designation along with your name.

In the past, many transgender folks have chosen to change their names by the usage method, perhaps to keep the matter out of the public record. Because we can't recommend the usage method in general anymore, we certainly can't recommend it for transgender people, either. In addition, given that transgender men and women face discrimination in so many areas of their lives, they will undoubtedly face resistance to efforts to change official records without a court order. For these reasons, and because there are new Judicial Council forms, we strongly recommend going ahead with your name and birth certificate change through the court petition process.

The court order for changing your name and recognizing your gender will allow you to change the gender designation that is listed on your original birth certificate and other official documents. You can also get court recognition of your gender change even if you don't change your name.

Terminology

The state-issued form that allows you to petition the court for an official name change and an order that your birth certificate be changed is called "Petition for Change of Name and Gender." This is something of a misnomer, because you have already changed your gender, so you are not actually asking the court to make you a different gender. More accurately, you are asking the court to recognize your change of gender for the purpose of correcting the gender designation on your birth certificate (to reflect your already-completed transition from one gender to the other). In this chapter, we will refer to "court recognition" of your gender, or to the resulting change in your "gender designation" rather than to the shorthand "change of gender" used on the court forms—except where we are referring to the forms, when we will use the title that the form uses, to avoid confusion.

To petition the court for a change of name and gender designation, you will use the special forms discussed in this chapter. You will also need to ask your doctor (or any doctor licensed in California, if your doctor is not) to sign a written declaration stating that you have transitioned from one gender to another and that surgery was a part of your transition. If you have not had any surgery as part of your transition, see "Gender Change Without Surgery," below.

SKIP AHEAD

If you've already changed your name and you only need court recognition of your gender so that you can change the gender designation on your birth certificate, skip ahead to "Getting Court Recognition of Your Gender When You Have Already Changed Your Name," below.

Forms for Change of Name and Gender

This section gives step-by-step instructions for completing the Judicial Council forms for changing your name and getting court recognition of your gender. There are four basic name and gender change forms, plus the Civil Case Cover Sheet, that you will file. If you need a waiver of court fees, there are additional forms, and those are discussed in Chapter 8.

Petition for Change of Name and Gender

Following are instructions for filling out the Judicial Council Petition for Change of Name and Gender.

CD-ROM

You'll find a blank copy of the Petition for Change of Name and Gender on the CD-ROM at the back of the book. You can also download the form at www.courtinfo. ca.gov/forms/fillable/nc200.pdf.

At the top of the first page of each form, you'll find several boxes with blank spaces, which together are the "caption." Here's how to fill it in:

Petitioner or Attorney. As the person filling out and filing the forms, you are the Petitioner. Fill in your present name in capital letters, followed by your mailing address and telephone number. You may also list your fax number and email address, if you wish. (The court will not use your email address to contact you, so if you want to keep it out of the public record, simply leave that line blank.) After "Attorney For," write "In Pro Per." (In fancy Latin language, this means you are representing yourself.)

Superior Court of California, County of. In capital letters, fill in the county in which you are filing your papers. In the spaces provided underneath, fill in the court's street address, mailing address, and city and zip code. Also fill in the branch name, if there is one.

Petition of (Names of each petitioner): Fill in your own present name in all capital letters.

Petition for Change of Name and Gender. This is the title of this particular form; each form has one. Leave the title as it is.

Case Number: This is the spot where the court clerk will write or stamp your case number when you file your papers. Leave this space blank for now. When you file your Petition, the clerk will open a file for you and assign you a case number. If you later need to file additional papers as part of this same name change petition, you'll need to use this number.

Item 1. Type your present name and your proposed name.

Item 2. Check the box indicating whether you are changing your gender designation from male to female or from female to male.

Items 3-5. You do not have to do anything with these items.

Item 6. You do not have to do anything on the Petition form related to this item, but you will need to attach both your physician's declaration and the Name and Information About the Person Whose Name Is to Be Changed attachment, described just below. For more about the physician declaration requirement, see "Gender Change Without Surgery," below.

You do not need to sign this Petition; you will sign on the attachment.

Name and Information Attachment

This is the form that gives the court all the pertinent information about you and your request for change of name and gender designation. Here are the instructions for filling out the Name and Information attachment.

CD-ROM

You'll find a blank copy of the Name and Information Sheet on the CD-ROM at the back of the book. You can also download the form at www.courtinfo.ca.gov/forms/nc110.pdf.

Caption. Fill in your present name in the box labeled "Petition Of." Leave the Case Number box blank. The court clerk will put your newly assigned case number here when you file your papers.

Item 6(b). Check the "self" box.

Item (1). Fill in your present name. If you have used a number of different names in the past, list the present name followed by the other names as AKAs (also known as).

Item (2). Fill in your proposed new name.

Item (3). Fill in your birth date and check the appropriate box to mark that you are 18 years of age or older.

Item (4). Fill in your city and state of birth—including the country if you were born outside of the United States (you need not be a citizen to have your name changed).

Item (5). Check the correct box for the sex that is stated on your original birth certificate.

Item (6). Fill in your complete current home address, including county. This must be the same county where you will be filing the name change papers. There is no time requirement for residency—it does not matter if you have lived in the county for one week or 20 years.

Item 6(c). Briefly state why you are seeking a name change. Because every adult has the legal right to change his or her name, the court should grant your Petition unless you are changing it for one of the prohibited reasons discussed in Chapter 3. Just state your reason as simply as possible. If you wish, you can simply type, "I have changed my gender and the new name is consistent with my changed gender identity." Or, if there are other reasons involved in your name change, such as taking an old family name, you can add that information as well. See the sidebar in Chapter 6, "Reasons for an Adult's Name Change," for examples of reasons for a name change.

Item 6(d). Check the box for "self."

Items 6(e) and (f). Leave these items blank.

Declaration. In the middle of the page there is a box with a separate signature line, where you will need to confirm that you are not in prison or on parole, and are not a registered sex offender. As noted above, if any of those things is true, you will need special permission to change your name. (See Chapter 6.) Check the appropriate boxes, print or type your name on the left-hand line, and sign on the signature line.

At the bottom of the form, date and sign the attachment where indicated, printing or typing your name next to the signature line. Sign your present name.

Declaration of Physician

The law that grants the court the power to recognize your post-transition gender states that you must have "undergone surgical treatment for the purpose of altering sexual characteristics to those of the opposite sex." (Cal Health & Safety Code § 103425.)

The statute does not specify what that surgical treatment has to be in order to meet this requirement. Attorneys who work regularly with transgender petitioners report that the courts are interpreting this language broadly to include any transition related surgery that changes sex characteristics.

The statute also requires that you submit a declaration from your surgeon along with your petition. The declaration informs the court that you have undergone surgery that changes sex characteristics. If your surgeon is unavailable, the declaration can also be from a physician who has examined you since your surgery.

The form that accomplishes this has the enormously long name "Declaration of Physician Documenting Change of Gender Through Surgical Treatment Under Health and Safety Code Sections 103425 and 103430."

CD-ROM

You can find a blank copy of this form on the CD-ROM at the back of the book. You can also download the form at www.courtinfo.ca.gov/forms/fillable/nc210.pdf.

Caption. Follow the directions above for filling out the abbreviated caption at the top of the page. Underneath the caption, include the number of pages included in your Petition, and which number this page is. For example, if your Petition includes, as it must, a Name and Information Attachment and a Declaration of Physician, then this Declaration page will be "Page 3 of 3."

Body of Declaration. You'll need to get your doctor to fill out the text required in this form. Here is some sample language that you can suggest to your doctor:

Sample Physician Declaration

I, James Richardson, declare:

1. I am a licensed physician in the state of California. I have personal and firsthand knowledge of the matters set forth herein and could competently testify thereto under oath.

2. Joe Nolo, whose date of birth is May 15, 19xx, is a patient of mine. On June 24, 20xx, I performed surgery on Joe Nolo that was an irreversible surgical procedure for the purpose of permanently transitioning from female to male. This procedure has changed Joe Nolo's sex characteristics. *[If a doctor other than the surgeon is writing the declaration, they can state that your medical records indicate that you have had surgery under the care of another doctor, and that they have examined you and can attest based on their examination and review of your records that you have undergone surgery that changed sex characteristics.]*

3. I declare under penalty of perjury under the laws of the State of California that the foregoing is true and correct and that this declaration is executed on April 4, 20xx, in San Francisco, California.

Date and Signature. Your doctor must date and sign this form.

If the judge asks you any questions about your surgery that you are uncomfortable answering, you can ask the judge for a continuance of your case and consult an attorney with expertise in this area before the date of the rescheduled hearing.

Order to Show Cause for Change of Name and Gender

This form is the official court document by which the court notifies anyone who may oppose your proposed name change and change of gender designation to come forward and voice their objection. In theory at least, the public will be aware of this order because you will publish it in the legal notices section of a local newspaper once a week for four weeks.

Instructions for publishing the Order to Show Cause are in Chapter 8. You can skip ahead to that chapter to figure out what newspaper you want to use, and then return to these instructions. Once you've selected a newspaper for publication according to the instructions in that chapter, you're ready to complete the form.

CD-ROM

You'll find a blank copy of the Order to Show Cause for Change of Name on the CD-ROM at the back of the book. You can also download the form at www.courtinfo.ca.gov/forms/fillable/nc220.pdf.

Caption. Follow the instructions above for filling out the caption.

Item 1. Fill in your present name in the space on the first line, and your proposed new name in the space on the second line.

Item 2. Check the appropriate box depending on whether you are changing your gender designation from male to female or from female to male.

Item 3. This line states that the court is ordering all persons who might want to object to your proposed name change and change of gender designation to appear at the court and voice their concerns at the time set for the hearing.

Item 3(a). Under the title "Notice of Hearing," the clerk will fill in the date and time of the hearing and the department and room number in which it will be held. Do not fill in the information requested in the box yourself.

Item 3(b). In the space provided, fill in the complete street address where the hearing will be held, unless it is the same as noted in the caption above.

Item 4. In this item, specify how you will publicize this order. If your county has at least one newspaper of general circulation that has been certified to publish legal notices, mark the box at (a). Write the complete name of the newspaper you have selected in the space provided. See Chapter 8 for information on selecting a newspaper. If your county does not have a paper that is certified to publish legal notices, check the box at (b) and ask the court clerk how to complete the following blank. See

Chapter 6 for information on contacting your court clerk.

Date and Judge's Signature. The judge will sign and date the Order here. Leave these items blank.

> **CAUTION**
>
> **If you don't want to publish the fact that you're seeking a gender change, consider using a different form.** This Order to Show Cause form, NC-220, specifies that you are seeking both a name and gender change, which means that your gender change request will become public knowledge along with your name change request. Some people doing gender changes argue that the gender change shouldn't be a required part of the publication, because there's no basis for anyone to object to it, as there might be with a name change. However, the Judicial Council has so far declined to change the form. The fact that there's a very slim likelihood of anyone ever seeing your legal announcement makes many people feel okay about publishing the Order to Show Cause as it is, but if you have concerns about it, you can try using NC-120, the Order to Show Cause for Change of Name, as the form that you publish. If you choose to go this route, you'll also need to ask the clerk to fill out a form NC-320, Notice of Hearing on Petition for Change of Gender and Issuance of New Birth Certificate, to be sure the record is clear that your hearing will cover both issues. (Instructions for filling out this form are in the section titled "Getting Court Recognition of Your Gender When You Have Already Changed Your Name,"

below.) If you're going to go this direction, you may need the assistance of an attorney—contact the Transgender Law Center at www.transgenderlawcenter.org.

Decree Changing Name and Gender

The Decree is the judge's order legally changing your name and recognizing your gender. Even though the Decree won't be signed until the very end of the process, you should complete it and give it to the court clerk along with the other papers. The clerk will not file the Decree, but will keep it in your file until the judge is ready to sign it (or, the clerk may give the Decree back to you to hold until the hearing date).

Here are instructions for completing the Decree Changing Name and Gender form.

CD-ROM

You'll find a blank copy of the Decree Changing Name and Gender on the CD-ROM at the back of the book. You can also download the form at www.courtinfo.ca.gov/forms/fillable/nc230.pdf.

Caption. Follow the instructions above for filling out the caption.

Item 1. Leave this sentence blank—the court clerk will fill in the date and courtroom of the hearing when the hearing is actually held.

Items 2(a)–(f). Leave these items blank—the judge will fill in the appropriate information. (Sometimes, the court clerk will have you fill it in on the day of the hearing—when you present the papers, ask the clerk whether you should fill it in or whether the judge will do it.)

Item 3. On these lines, fill in your present name and your proposed new name.

Item 4. Fill in your new name on the top line, and check either box (a) or (b), depending on whether you are changing your gender designation from female to male or from male to female.

Item 5. You need not do anything with this item.

Date and Judge's Signature. The judge will sign and date the Decree here. Leave these items blank.

Civil Case Cover Sheet

All courts will require you to file a form called the "Civil Case Cover Sheet" with the rest of your documents. This form simply says that you are petitioning to change your name, so the clerk can easily see what your case is about. This form should be filed with the court at the same time as your Petition for Change of Name and Gender.

Because this form should be filled out the same way in all name change petitions, except of course for the caption information personal to you, we have filled out much of this form for you.

⊙ **CD-ROM**
You can find a partially filled-out copy on the CD-ROM at the back of the book. You can also download the form at www.courtinfo.ca.gov/forms/fillable/cm010.pdf.

If you use the tear-out form we have provided, you need only type in the following information.

Caption. Follow the directions above for filling out the caption. Fill in your personal information, the court information, and the case name as you have done on every other form.

Date and Signature. At the bottom of the page, fill in the date and your present name, then sign the form.

Gender Change Without Surgery

If you have changed your gender but have not had any kind of surgery as a part of your transition (and don't intend to do so), you will have more difficulty getting a court to recognize your gender change. You will still be able to change your name using the method described in Chapter 6, but whether the court will order that your birth certificate be changed (an order that you can also use to change other official records) will probably depend on what your doctor will write in a declaration and how sympathetic the judge is.

If your doctor will declare under penalty of perjury that you have fully transitioned to your new gender without surgery, and the judge is very sympathetic to your situation, you may be able to get a court order recognizing your gender and ordering the Office of Vital Records to change the gender designation on your birth certificate. However, because of the requirement of surgical intervention, this may be a losing battle. If, as is likely, you cannot persuade a court to order your birth certificate changed without verification of surgical gender reassignment, you will have to either settle for changing only your name, or try to be a test case and pursue the matter through a court appeal or some kind of legislative action. To do either of these things, you will want to consult an attorney. See Chapter 11 for more information about hiring an attorney, and see below for other resources.

Alternatives to Court Recognition of Your Gender Change

If you aren't able to get court recognition of your gender, there are other things that you can do to have your gender designation changed on some official documents. For example, the DMV will change the gender designation on your driver's license or California ID card if you file form DL-329, Medical Certification and Authorization (Gender Change). The form must be signed by a physician or psychologist, stating that your gender has changed. This may seem odd, given the restrictiveness of the gender

A Public Service Agency

MEDICAL CERTIFICATION AND AUTHORIZATION
(Gender Change)

SECTION 1 – APPLICANT'S TRUE FULL NAME (TO BE COMPLETED BY THE APPLICANT)

LAST	FIRST	MIDDLE	DATE OF BIRTH (MM,DD,YYYY)
Nolo	Joe	Jakne	05/15/1984

MAILING ADDRESS	CITY	STATE	ZIP CODE	CALIFORNIA DRIVER LICENSE/IDENTIFICATION CARD NUMBER
1212 Laurel Street	Anywhere	CA	94123	N1234567

RESIDENCE ADDRESS (IF DIFFERENT FROM MAILING ADDRESS)	CITY	STATE	ZIP CODE
same as above			

DAYTIME TELEPHONE NUMBER	SOCIAL SECURITY NUMBER
(510)555-1212	123-45-6789

SECTION 2 – CERTIFICATION

I certify (or declare) under penalty of perjury under the laws of the State of California that the foregoing is true and correct.

APPLICANT SIGNATURE	DATE
X *Joe Nolo*	12/3/20xx

AUTHORIZATION

All records of the department relating to the physical or mental condition of any person are confidential and not open to public inspection per California Vehicle Code Section 1808.5.

I hereby authorize my physician/psychologist, or health service provider, to release the information below to the California Department of Motor Vehicles for the purpose of obtaining a driver license or an identification card under my preferred gender. ___*JN*___ (Applicant's Initials)

SECTION 3 – TO BE COMPLETED BY A PHYSICIAN/PSYCHOLOGIST LICENSED IN THE UNITED STATES

My professional opinion is that the applicant's:

Gender identification is: [X] Male [ ] Female

Demeanor is: [X] Male [ ] Female

Only a physician licensed in the United States can certify that gender identification is complete.

Gender identification is: [X] Complete [ ] Transitional

SECTION 4 – TO BE COMPLETED BY A PHYSICIAN/PSYCHOLOGIST LICENSED IN THE UNITED STATES

FULL NAME OF PHYSICIAN/PSYCHOLOGIST (PRINT)
Jack Jones

[X] Physician [ ] Psychologist	EXAMINATION DATE	MEDICAL CASE NUMBER
	12/3/20xx	1234

EMAIL ADDRESS
drjones@gmail.com

MEDICAL LICENSE OR CERTIFICATE NUMBER	ISSUING STATE	TELEPHONE NUMBER
34568	CA	(415)555-1212

NAME OF HOSPITAL OR MEDICAL CLINIC
San Francisco Medical Group

MAILING ADDRESS	CITY	STATE	ZIP CODE
1234 Market Street	San Francisco	CA	94110

PHYSICAL ADDRESS (IF DIFFERENT FROM MAILING ADDRESS) CITY STATE ZIP CODE
N/A

SECTION 5 – CERTIFICATION

I certify (or declare) under penalty of perjury under the laws of the State of California that the foregoing is true and correct.

SIGNATURE OF PHYSICIAN OR PSYCHOLOGIST	DATE
X *Jack Jones*	12/3/20xx

SECTION 6 – FOR DMV USE ONLY

DMV MANAGER OR DESIGNEE'S SIGNATURE:	DATE LINE STAMP
X	

This form is void five (5) years from the date of the physician or psychologist certification.

DL 329 (NEW 8/2008) WWW

change statute, but for purposes of the DMV form it appears that not only can you get a gender change on your license without having had any surgery, but you also do not even need to have received any medical treatment as part of your transition. All that's required is that you have consulted with a doctor and the doctor has examined you.

 CD-ROM

A blank copy of the form is included on the CD-ROM at the back of the book. A sample of the DL-329 is shown above, filled out to demonstrate how you would complete the form. A few specific instructions follow.

Section 1. Fill in your name, address, telephone number, and identifying information—birth date, drivers' license number, and Social Security number.

Section 2. Sign and date the form.

Section 3. Your doctor will fill in this portion of the form. The DMV may reject the form if this section is not filled out completely, so make sure that one of the boxes on each of the top three lines is checked.

If your doctor isn't sure whether to check the "complete" box, especially if you haven't had surgery, you can remind the doctor that you are expressing your gender identity full-time, a consistency that renders your change complete. If any questions come up, suggest that your doctor contact the Transgender Law Center (www.transgenderlawcenter.org). If the

doctor does check the "transitional" box, you'll have to submit another DL-329 every five years, and if you don't, your original gender marker will be restored in your DMV records. Finally, only a physician, not a psychologist, can certify that your gender change is complete.

Sections 4-6. Your doctor must fill in the information requested in Section 4, and sign and date the form in Section 5. Make sure the doctor puts "M.D." or "Ph.D." after the signature. Section 6 is for DMV use.

TIP

Call the DMV if you have problems. If you run into any trouble filing the form after following these instructions (which were prepared in consultation with the DMV), you can call the DMV records security division for assistance, at 916-657-6613.

Armed with your new driver's license or ID card, you should be able to get nongovernmental records, such as school and medical records, changed to reflect your new gender designation. However, dealing with government agencies may be a different story, and different agencies have different policies—you should check with each agency about what it requires.

Getting Court Recognition of Your Gender When You Have Already Changed Your Name

While you can petition a court to change your name and officially recognize your gender at the same time, you aren't required to do both together. If you have already officially changed your name or don't need to change your name, you can petition a court for recognition of your gender only, and ask for an order that your birth certificate be changed as well.

Petition for Change of Gender and Issuance of New Birth Certificate

This is the form you will use if you want to change your gender designation but not your name.

CD-ROM

You'll find a blank copy of the Petition for Change of Gender on the CD-ROM at the back of the book. You can also download the form at www.courtinfo.ca.gov/forms/fillable/nc300.pdf.

Caption. The top third of the form is called the "caption." You can find instructions for filling out the caption under the section "Petition for Change of Name and Gender," above.

Item 1. Type your present name.

Item 2. Check the box indicating whether you are changing your gender designation from male to female or from female to male.

Item 3. You do not have to do anything on the Petition form related to this item, but you will need to attach a declaration from your physician. That form is discussed below.

Item 4. Check the box indicating whether or not you have obtained a name change. If you changed your name in connection with your gender change, attach a copy of the order changing your name.

Item 5. You do not need to do anything with this item.

Date and signature. Date and sign the form where indicated, printing your name next to your signature.

Declaration of Physician

The law that grants the court the power to recognize your post-transition gender states that you must have "undergone surgical treatment for the purpose of altering sexual characteristics to those of the opposite sex." (Cal Health & Safety Code § 103425.) The statute does not specify what that surgical treatment has to be in order to meet this requirement. Attorneys who work regularly with transgender petitioners report that the courts are interpreting this language broadly to include any transition-related surgery that changes sex characteristics.

The statute also requires that you submit a declaration from your surgeon along with your petition. The declaration informs the court that you have undergone surgery that changes sex characteristics. If your surgeon is unavailable, the declaration can also be from a physician who has examined you since your surgery.

The form that accomplishes this has the long name "Declaration of Physician Documenting Change of Gender Through Surgical Treatment Under Health and Safety Code Sections 103425 and 103430."

CD-ROM

You can find a blank copy of this form on the CD-ROM at the back of the book. You can also download the form at www. courtinfo.ca.gov/forms/fillable/nc210.pdf.

Follow the instructions for filling out this form in the section on "Forms for Change of Name and Gender," above.

Notice of Hearing on Petition for Change of Gender and Issuance of New Birth Certificate

You don't have to publish notice that you're asking for a legal gender change and a new birth certificate, like you do when you're changing your name. But you do have a complete and file a Notice of Hearing with the court.

CD-ROM

You'll find a blank copy of the Notice of Hearing on Petition for Change of Gender and Issuance of New Birth Certificate on the CD-ROM at the back of the book. You can also download the form at www.courtinfo.ca.gov/forms/fillable/nc320.pdf.

Caption. The top third of the form is called the "caption." You can find instructions for filling out the caption under the section "Petition for Change of Name and Gender," above.

Item 1. Type your present name.

Item 2. Check the box indicating whether you are changing your gender designation from male to female or from female to male.

Item 3a. It's possible that the clerk will keep the Notice of Hearing and mail it to you when the court date has been set and the judge has signed the form. It's also possible (and somewhat more likely) that the clerk will stamp it with a judge's signature stamp, write a date in the date box, and give it back to you right then. Follow the clerk's lead on this one.

Item 3b. If the location of your hearing is the same as the address you listed in the caption, check the first box. If it's not, check the second box and type in the location of the hearing.

Item 4. It's unlikely you'll have anything to include under Item 4. Leave it blank unless the clerk advises you there's something else that needs to be included there.

Date and signature. Leave this section blank. The clerk will take care of it.

Order for Change of Gender and Issuance of New Birth Certificate

The final step in asking the court to change your gender designation and order the issuance of a new birth certificate is to submit an order for the judge's signature.

CD-ROM

You'll find a blank copy of the Order for Change of Gender and Issuance of New Birth Certificate on the CD-ROM at the back of the book. You can also download the form at www.courtinfo.ca.gov/forms/fillable/nc330.pdf.

Caption. The top third of the form is called the "caption." You can find instructions for filling out the caption under the section "Petition for Change of Name and Gender," above.

Item 1. Type your present name and the date of your hearing, if you know it. If you're submitting the form in advance and you don't yet know the hearing date, leave that part blank for the clerk to fill in later.

Item 2. Leave this item blank for the clerk or judge to complete.

Item 3. Check the box indicating whether you are changing your gender designation from male to female or from female to male.

Items 4 and 5. There's nothing you need to do with these items, which are the court's orders.

Date and signature. Leave this section blank for the judge to date and sign.

Civil Case Cover Sheet

You will need to submit a Civil Case Cover Sheet along with your other documents, regardless of whether you use modified Judicial Council forms or forms that you prepare yourself. See "Civil Case Cover Sheet," above, for instructions on preparing the Civil Case Cover Sheet.

Filing Your Petition, Publishing Your Order to Show Cause, and Obtaining Your Order

For instructions on the nitty-gritty of getting your Petition filed with the court, getting your Order to Show Cause published, and getting the court to sign the Decree Changing Name and Gender or the Decree Changing Gender alone, see Chapter 8. Then return to the following section for instructions on how to get a new birth certificate.

TIP

Publication is required if you're changing your name and gender, but not your gender only. Publication is usually in such an obscure section of the paper that most people aren't too concerned about the requirement. And a gender change without a name change doesn't require publication.

Obtaining a New Birth Certificate

To obtain a new California birth certificate, you will need to send a form requesting a new birth certificate; a certified copy of the Decree Changing Name and Gender

If You Were Born Outside of California

If you were born outside of California, you will need to contact the state where you were born and find out its procedures for changing birth certificates after court recognition of a gender change. You should be able to find the phone number for the department of vital statistics in your birth state by searching the Internet, then call to find out what is required for a birth certificate change. In some states, you may be able to send only a surgeon's letter. In others, you will need to send a certified copy of the Decree Changing Name and Gender or the Decree Changing Gender. And states differ in how they do amendments. Some will issue a new birth certificate, while others will only prepare an attachment for your original birth certificate.

Under the United States Constitution, all states are bound to recognize orders of superior courts in any other state. This means that in theory, armed with your order from a California judge, you should be able to get a new birth certificate no matter where you were born. However, a few states have policies or even laws that prohibit court recognition of gender changes.

The constitutionality of these policies has not yet been challenged, so in those states you may not be able to amend your birth certificate unless you're willing to be a test case. Of course, you should first check with the state to find out whether they will change your birth certificate; if they refuse because they have a policy as described above, contact a lawyer to see what your options are.

In other states, even where gender changes are recognized by the courts, you may run into a bureaucrat who is reluctant to amend your birth certificate because of ignorance or prejudice. If this happens, ask to speak to the person's supervisor, and go up the ladder until you find someone who will help you. If you continue to run into problems, you will probably need to consult with an attorney. Contact the Transgender Law Center at www.transgenderlawcenter.org to find a lawyer who can help.

or the Decree Changing Gender, signed by the judge; and the correct fee to the Office of Vital Records (OVR).

The form for amending your birth certificate is called Affidavit to Amend a Record; its number is VS-24. A sample of the form, borrowed from the OVR website, is shown below, filled out to demonstrate how you would complete the form to change your name and/or gender designation, along with instructions on how to fill it out. This form is not included in the appendix, because you cannot use a photocopy of the form when you submit your application to the Office of Vital Records. Instead, you must obtain the original form from the OVR.

You can get the Affidavit to Amend a Record at www.apps.cdph.ca.gov or by calling 916-445-2684; you can also get a copy from your local County Health Department or county recorder (this will be the fastest way to get it). See the OVR website at www.dph.ca.gov for answers to frequently asked questions, more information about ordering forms, and fee information. The OVR also has a new pamphlet called "Obtaining a New Birth Certificate After Gender Reassignment" that you can download from the website. To contact the OVR in writing, write to Office of Vital Records, Department of Public Health, MS 5103, P.O. Box 997410, Sacramento, CA 95899-7410, 916-445-2684.

Here's how to fill out the Affidavit to Amend a Record after a change of name and gender.

Top section. Check the box next to "birth" under the title "Affidavit to Amend a Record." Leave the lines to either side of that box blank.

Part I: Information to Locate Record. The second part of the form tells the OVR how to find your birth record, so it must include the information that is on your original birth certificate. If you don't know this information, and you need a copy of your original birth certificate, you can obtain one from the OVR or from the County Recorder in the county where you were born. The County Recorder will be able to give you a copy of the original birth certificate much more quickly than the OVR. It's helpful to the OVR clerks if you send a photocopy of your original birth certificate, if you have it.

 CAUTION

It's very important that you fill in the form on a typewriter or use a black pen—no other color of ink will be accepted. It's also a good idea to get more than one copy of the form when you order it from OVR (they're free), in case you make a mistake. The form will not be accepted if it has any erasures, cross-outs, white-outs, or alterations.

Items 1A–1C. Type or write in the full name that was given to you at birth. In the sample, the person's first and middle names were not registered and that's what the person is trying to correct.

Item 2. Type or write in the sex that was listed on your original birth certificate.

Item 3. Type or write in your birth date.

Items 4–5. Type or write in the city and county of your birth.

Item 6. Type or write in your father's name as it was stated on your original birth certificate.

Item 7. Type or write in your mother's name as it was stated on your original birth certificate.

Part II: Statement of Corrections. This is where you will enter the new information.

Item 8. List the item number (from Part 1) for each item that needs to be changed. (The sample shows a change of name; if you are changing your gender as well, include that on its own line.)

Item 9. List the information that needs to be changed as it appears on your original birth record.

Item 10. Enter the information as it should appear on your new birth record.

Item 11. As your reason for the correction, enter the superior court information from your name and/or gender change petition. Give only the relevant details, and leave some space blank in case the OVR needs to enter additional information.

Item 12A. Sign the form here. Use your current legal name after the name change.

Item 12B. Type your name here.

Item 12C. Insert the word "self."

Items 12D–12E. Put in your address and the date that you are signing the form.

Items 13A–13E. You must have a second person sign the form, essentially as a witness to confirm the information you've included. You could use a relative or a friend as long as the person knew you before the gender change. Insert the requested information, which is the same as what was requested of you above, in items 13A through 13E.

CAUTION

Don't believe everything you read. The version of the form that was current at the time this book went to press says that your original birth certificate will not be altered (in the general information section on the back of the form). This is not true. OVR will issue a new birth certificate after a change of name and gender designation. Your original birth certificate will be sealed (no one will have access to it but you, unless they have a court order), and the new birth certificate will have no reference to the gender and name change or to the fact that you once had a different name and gender designation.

After you have finished filling out the form, make sure that you attach a certified copy of the Decree Changing Name and Gender or Decree Changing Gender, and the correct fees. Send the form to the address listed on the back of the form. It may take up to a year to get your new birth certificate.

Obtaining a New Passport

Until recently, the U.S. State Department required proof of surgical sex reassignment to issue a new passport. New rules provide that applicants for a gender marker change on their passports do not need to show proof of surgical intervention. Instead, they must submit certification from a physician that they have received "appropriate clinical treatment" for gender transition.

If you have a passport that is still valid but does not reflect your current gender, follow the instructions in Chapter 10 for getting a new passport after a name change, and attach a letter from your doctor certifying that you've received the required treatment.

RESOURCE

For more information about legal issues involved in gender transition, you can contact the Transgender Law Center in San Francisco at 415-865-0176 (www.transgender lawcenter.org).

AFFIDAVIT TO AMEND A RECORD
NO ERASURES, WHITEOUTS, PHOTOCOPIES, OR ALTERATIONS

[X] BIRTH   [ ] DEATH   [ ] FETAL DEATH

TYPE OR PRINT CLEARLY IN BLACK INK ONLY – THIS AMENDMENT BECOMES AN ACTUAL PART OF THE OFFICIAL RECORD

PART I   INFORMATION TO LOCATE RECORD

INFORMATION AS IT APPEARS ON ORIGINAL RECORD	1A. NAME—FIRST	1B. MIDDLE		1C. LAST
	--	--		Doe

	2. SEX	3. DATE OF EVENT—MM/DD/CCYY	4. CITY OF EVENT	5. COUNTY OF EVENT
	Male	05/12/2005	Sacramento	Sacramento

6. FULL NAME OF FATHER/PARENT AS STATED ON ORIGINAL RECORD	7. FULL NAME OF MOTHER/PARENT AS STATED ON ORIGINAL RECORD
John -- Doe	Mary Jane Smith

PART II   STATEMENT OF CORRECTIONS TO BIRTH, DEATH, OR FETAL DEATH RECORD

LIST ONE ITEM PER LINE

8. ITEM NUMBER TO BE CORRECTED	9. INCORRECT INFORMATION THAT APPEARS ON ORIGINAL RECORD	10. CORRECTED INFORMATION AS IT SHOULD APPEAR
1A	--	John
1B	--	Michael
10	LA	CA

11. REASON FOR CORRECTION: To add child's first and middle names and correct mother's state of birth to California

---

AFFIDAVITS AND SIGNATURES

TWO PERSONS MUST SIGN THIS FORM TO CORRECT A BIRTH, DEATH, OR FETAL DEATH RECORD

We, the undersigned, hereby certify under penalty of perjury that we have personal knowledge of the above facts and that the information given above is true and correct.

12A. SIGNATURE OF FIRST PERSON	12B. PRINTED NAME	12C. TITLE/RELATIONSHIP TO PERSON IN PART I
▶ *John Doe*	John Doe	Self

12D. ADDRESS (STREET and NUMBER, CITY, STATE, ZIP)	12E. DATE SIGNED—MM/DD/CCYY
1234 Main Street, Sacramento, CA 95817	01/05/20xx

13A. SIGNATURE OF SECOND PERSON	13B. PRINTED NAME	13C. TITLE/RELATIONSHIP TO PERSON IN PART I
▶ *Mary Jane Smith-Doe*	Mary Jane Smith-Doe	Mother

13D. ADDRESS (STREET and NUMBER, CITY, STATE, ZIP)	13E. DATE SIGNED—MM/DD/CCYY
1234 Main Street, Sacramento, CA 95817	01/05/20xx

STATE/LOCAL REGISTRAR USE ONLY

14. OFFICE OF VITAL RECORDS OR LOCAL REGISTRAR	15. DATE ACCEPTED FOR REGISTRATION
▶	

STATE OF CALIFORNIA, DEPARTMENT OF PUBLIC HEALTH, OFFICE OF VITAL RECORDS   FORM VS 24 (REV. 1/08)

Filing, Publishing, and Serving Your Court Petition

Now that your papers are in order, it's time to file them with the court and get your name change application underway. Whether you are petitioning for your own name change, for a change of name and gender designation, or to change a minor's name, the basic instructions are the same. In this chapter, we take you through the details of the court petition process, including:

- checking the formatting and filing rules that make up the nitty-gritty requirements for how papers must be filed
- copying and filing your papers with the court
- arranging to have your Order to Show Cause published in a local newspaper, and
- if you are filing on behalf of a child without the child's other parent or parents, serving the Order to Show Cause on the child's relatives.

File Papers With the Court

To get your Court Petition started, you will have to file your papers with the superior court clerk in your county and pay a filing fee.

Instructions for Filing

"Filing" your papers means submitting them to the court and having them officially entered in your court file. To file your documents, start by making at

---

> ### Check the Rules of Court Before Filing
>
> In the past, each local court could make up its own rules about how papers needed to be filed. These rules related to everything from how many copies you were required to file to whether you were allowed to fold your documents before filing them. They sometimes ended up seeming like a trap for self-represented parties who might end up having to do something over if they didn't comply with their county's particular rules. Now, local counties are no longer allowed to make their own rules. Instead, the Judicial Council is in charge of making all the rules about the format of papers, and you can find all those rules in one place, in California Rules of Court 2.100 and following. You can find the California Rules of Court at www.courtinfo.ca.gov/rules.

least three photocopies of each of the documents you've prepared. Even if the court requires you to file only the original, it's a good idea to have extra copies. For one thing, you will want file-stamped copies to keep for your records. Also, if you are seeking a name change for your child and the child's other parent is not signing the petition, you'll definitely need extra copies of the documents. Finally, if there is no newspaper that publishes legal notices in your county, you'll need to file three extra copies of the Order to Show Cause. (See below for information on having your Order to Show Cause published.) If a form has attachments, staple the attachments to the form.

To file your documents, take or send them to the superior court clerk. Whether you file in person or by mail, be sure to include:

- the original documents
- the correct number of copies of each document, and
- the correct filing fee or your fee waiver documents. (In Chapter 1 you learned that fees are around $250–300. See below for fee waiver information.)

If you file by mail, also include two self-addressed, stamped envelopes.

TIP

File in person if you are in a hurry. If you have left something out or made a small mistake, the clerk will tell you and you may be able to fix it right then and there. If you file by mail, you lose time while the papers are being mailed back and forth.

If you mail the documents, include an explanatory cover letter. (A sample letter is shown below.) Regardless of whether you file your papers in person or mail them, it's a good idea to leave an extra copy (or two) of everything at home, in case the papers are misplaced.

When you deliver your papers to the court, the clerk will open a new file and assign your case a number. This number will be written or stamped on all of your documents. The clerk will file your Civil Case Cover Sheet form and Petition form

and may keep one or two photocopies. Any extra copies will be returned to you. They will have a stamp in the upper right-hand corner, showing the date that the original was filed.

The clerk will also assign a court hearing date for the judge to consider your case—usually about six weeks from the date you file your papers, but sometimes much longer in large, busy counties. In some larger counties, you may have to get the court date from a different person, called the "calendar clerk." If you can't appear at the date and time the clerk selects, ask the clerk for a different hearing date. (Another good reason to file in person if you can.) The clerk will write the date, time, and location of the hearing in the appropriate box on the Order to Show Cause.

TIP

If you are filing a petition to change a minor's name, and the other parent does not agree to the name change, you will have to serve the other parent. If you don't know the other parent's whereabouts and you will have to do a search as described in "Publishing Notice to the Other Parent," below, ask the clerk to set a hearing date that will give you enough time to make a search, ask the court for permission to publish notice, and publish notice for four weeks. The date should probably be at least ten to 12 weeks away. Likewise, if you know where the other parent lives but you still think you might have trouble with service, ask for some extra time (and remember, the papers must be served at least 30 days before the hearing).

In addition to filing your papers, you need to get the Order to Show Cause signed by a judge. (It can't be published until it's signed.) The court will probably have a procedure in place for you to accomplish this on the day you file your papers. For example, when you call the clerk for information you may be told that a judge is available at a certain time each day to sign orders, and that it's best to show up then to get your papers filed and signed. In other counties, the clerk of the court will take your Order to Show Cause and present it to a judge for signing at a later time. You can either leave a self-addressed, stamped envelope with the clerk to have the Order to Show Cause sent to you, or make arrangements to come back later and pick up the signed copy. When the judge signs the Order, the court will officially file it and you can then have the file-stamped copy published in the paper.

When you hand in or mail your Decree Changing Name to the clerk, the clerk will keep it, but not officially file it. It will be filed after your name change is approved and signed by the judge. (This usually occurs on your hearing date, whether a hearing is actually held or not.) In some courts, the clerk may enter your case number and then give the Decree right back to you for you to keep until your hearing date. But for your convenience, other courts will keep the Decree in your file until your petition is approved and the Decree is needed.

Sample Letter Accompanying Mailed Documents

November 11, 20xx

County Clerk
Superior Court of California
County of San Diego
P.O. Box 128
San Diego, CA 92112-4104

Dear Clerk:

I have enclosed:

1) An original and 4 copies each of:
   Civil Case Cover Sheet;
   Petition for Change of Name (including Name and Information About the Person Whose Name Is to Be Changed);
   Order to Show Cause; and
   Decree Changing Name.

2) A check in the amount of $355.00, and

3) Two self-addressed, stamped envelopes.

Please have the Order to Show Cause signed, file the first three documents, set a hearing date, and return file-stamped copies to me in one of the enclosed self-addressed, stamped envelopes. [Please set the hearing date no earlier than February 1, 20xx, as I will need time to publish notice to the other parent.] The second envelope is included for mailing a copy of the decree to me after it is signed at the hearing and filed.

Sincerely,

Bessie Johnson

Bessie Johnson

1 Main Street
San Diego, CA 92101
Daytime Phone: 619-555-0505

Applying for Waiver of Court Filing Fees and Costs

Under state rules, the court will waive your filing fees if you have a very low income and cannot afford to pay. You do not have to be destitute, but you really must be unable to pay—just hoping to avoid one more expense isn't good enough.

SKIP AHEAD

If you are able to pay the filing fee without any problem, or know that you do not qualify for a fee waiver, skip ahead to "Arrange for Publication of the Order to Show Cause," below.

According to the state's "Information Sheet on Waiver of Court Fees and Costs," you are automatically eligible for a waiver if:

- you are receiving public benefits
- your income is not enough to pay your household's basic needs and also pay court fees, or
- your total gross monthly household income (your monthly income before taxes or deductions are taken out) is equal to or less than the amounts shown in the chart below, "Qualifying Income for Waiver of Court Fees and Costs."

All fee waiver forms and documentation that you submit to the court are confidential. No one except court personnel has access to these papers without your permission.

Qualifying Income for Waiver of Court Fees and Costs

Use this chart to determine whether you qualify for a waiver of court fees.

Number in Family	Monthly Family Income
1	$1,128.13
2	$1,517.71
3	$1,907.30
4	$2,296.88
5	$2,686.46
6	$3,076.05
Each additional, add	$389.59

The figures on the fee waiver chart are from the Judicial Council's "Request to Waive Court Fees," revised July 2009, and were current when this book went to press. Check with the clerk to make sure the form—and the amounts listed—are up to date. This form, like the other forms we describe here, is available on the Judicial Council's website at www.courtinfo.ca.gov/forms/documents/fw001.pdf or from your local superior court. There is also a copy on the CD-ROM at the back of the book.

If your monthly income is higher than indicated in the chart but you nevertheless believe you can't afford to pay court fees, the court has discretion to waive your fees. But in this situation, you must provide information about your monthly expenses to demonstrate that you can't afford to pay. A judge will review your financial situation and decide whether all or part of the court expenses will be waived.

To apply, fill out two forms: a "Request to Waive Court Fees" and an "Order on Court Fee Waiver." The latter form will be signed by the judge if your application is approved. You will also need to supply proof of each of your statements to qualify for the waiver. We describe how to fill out these forms below.

You should normally file your fee waiver request at the same time you file your Petition for Change of Name. Some clerks may tell you that you'll have to wait a few days for a judge to grant the fee waiver before you can file your papers. If this happens, be polite but firm. Tell the clerk that you are entitled to file your Petition immediately under Rule 985(a) of the California Rules of Court, which states, "Upon the receipt of an application [for fee waiver], the clerk shall immediately file the application and any pleading or other paper presented by the applicant." If for some reason the clerk still will not file your papers, ask to speak with a supervisor. You can read Rule 985 in full on the Judicial Council's website, at www.courtinfo.ca.gov, in the Rules section of the site.

If you file your papers in person, allow a little extra time, as you may have to file the Request to Waive Court Fees application in a different department (courtroom) than the regular filing desk. To find out the procedure for filing fee waiver documents, check with the court clerk.

The court has five working days from the date you file to decide whether to grant your request for a fee waiver. If the court doesn't rule on your request within that period, your fees and costs are automatically waived. (Rule 985(e).) When the court rules on your application, it will complete the Order on Court Fee Waiver that you already filed, making it clear whether it has granted or denied your request. If the court grants your request, it might also file an additional document called "Notice of Waiver of Court Fees and Costs." However, some courts don't use this form. (The clerk is only required to use it if your application is granted because of the court's failure to act within five days.) If the court denies your application, you will have ten days to pay the filing fee for your name change petition or ask for a hearing. (See "Request for Hearing," below.)

If the court finds the information that you submitted confusing, and can't make a decision without talking to you, the order will say so, and will schedule a date when you must appear for a hearing no later than ten days away. The hearing will be a private meeting with the judge where you can explain your situation so that the judge can make a decision.

If the court waives your fees and costs, you will not be required to pay the filing fee for your Petition or other related court costs. However, the court waiver will not take care of the fee for publication of your documents in a local newspaper. You will still be responsible for that fee.

If, after the court grants your fee waiver application but before the court rules on your Petition, your finances improve and you no longer qualify, the law requires you to notify the court and pay your fees. (Rule 985(g).)

Request to Waive Court Fees

This form is your official request to the court to waive your fees and costs. In it, you will explain why you cannot pay court fees, and request that the court consider your name change Petition despite your inability to pay.

 CD-ROM

You'll find a blank copy of the Request to Waive Court Fees on the CD-ROM at the back of the book. You can also download the form at www.courtinfo.ca.gov/forms/fillable/fw001.pdf.

Caption. For this form, the caption is abbreviated. On the right in the second box from the top, put the court information. Fill in the case number just below (the clerk will complete it when your case number is assigned). Under "Case Name," write or type "Name change of [your current name]."

Item 1. Put your name and address as indicated.

Item 2. If you are employed, fill in your occupation, employer, and employer's address. If unemployed, fill in "N/A."

Item 3. Type the words "In Pro Per" on the first line.

Item 4. This item is already completed. You don't need to do anything.

Item 5. You will check one of the three boxes under item 5.

Item 5a. If you are receiving one of the types of public assistance listed under item 5a, check the main box and the box for the type(s) of assistance you receive, then skip items 5b and 5c. If you check this box, you won't need to complete any part of the second page of the form. You can skip to item 6 and then sign the form.

Item 5b. If your family income is less than the amounts listed under this item, check the box for this item. You'll need to fill out items 7, 8, and 9 on the second page of the form.

Item 5c. If you don't qualify for a fee waiver under either of the other criteria, but you don't have enough money to pay all of your court fees and still pay your household expenses, you can submit your income and expense information and ask the court to waive your fees on that basis. Check box "c" and then check one of the other boxes, depending on whether you want the court to waive all court fees, waive some court fees, or allow you to make payments over time. On the line that says "Explain," insert the words "see page 2," and then complete all of the items on page 2 (instructions below).

Item 6. It's unlikely you will need to check this box, but if you have filed a previous fee waiver request in the past six months, check the box and, if you have a copy of that previous request, check the second box and attach it.

Date and signature. Fill in the date and your present name and sign the form.

SKIP AHEAD

If you are on public assistance and you filled in Item 5a, do not complete the rest of the numbered items on this form. Jump to the date at the bottom of the front page, print or type your present name in the space provided at the left, and sign the form on the signature line. That's it—the form is ready for filing.

Caption on Page 2. Fill in your name and the name of any other Petitioner filing with you. Leave the case number blank because it won't be assigned until you file your Petition for Change of Name.

Item 7. Check this box if the amount of your earnings fluctuates from month to month, such as might occur if you are self-employed and make a fair amount of money one month but very little another month. If you check this item, use averages for each of the figures required in Item 8. For example, to get a monthly average of your income for the last year, add up your total earnings for the last 12 months and divide that amount by 12.

Item 8a. Fill in the amount of your gross monthly pay. This is the income you receive each month before any taxes or deductions are taken out.

Items 8a(1)–(4). Fill in the type and amount of each of your payroll deductions in the spaces provided. Then add together all of the amounts you listed and fill in the total payroll deduction amount.

Item 8b. Total your payroll deductions on this line.

Item 8c. Subtract the total payroll deductions from your gross monthly pay: Item 8a minus Item 8b. Fill in this amount.

Items 8d(1)–(4). Fill in information about other money you get each month, such as spousal support. Then fill in the total amount of additional money you receive each month after adding together the amounts you listed in Items 8d(1)–(4).

Item 8e. Add together Items 8c and 8d and enter this amount.

Items 9a(1)–(4). Fill in the total number of people living in your home and list their names, ages, relationships to you, and income, if any. Then add up the total.

Item 9b. Total the figures in 8e and 9b to get your total household income.

Items 10a–e. List the amount of cash you have, together with major assets as specified, with values and obligations.

Items 11a–m. In these items, tell how much you pay each month in living expenses. Make sure you list all of your expenses. List the total of all these expenses at the bottom of the column where indicated.

If there is any other reason why you can't pay court fees and costs, check the box inside the box at the bottom left side of the page, and follow the instructions there. This might include unusual medical expenses; money spent for a recent family emergency, such as funeral and burial expenses for an indigent parent; or travel to visit a seriously ill relative. You can use the Judicial Council Attachment form, mc-025. A blank copy is on the CD-ROM at the back of the book, and you can get a copy online at www.courtinfo.ca.gov/forms/fillable/mc025.pdf. In your own words, explain why you cannot pay the court fees and costs.

Order on Court Fee Waiver

This form, when signed by a judge, will be the document that officially orders your fees and costs to be waived. Following are the instructions for filling out the Order on Application for Waiver of Court Fees and Costs.

CD-ROM

You'll find a blank copy of the Order on Court Fee Waiver on the CD-ROM at the back of the book. You can also download the form at www.courtinfo.ca.gov/forms/fillable/fw003.pdf.

Caption. Put the court information in the second box on the right. Leave the "Case Number" box blank.

Item 1. Fill in your present name and your address.

Item 2. Fill in the words "In Pro Per" on the first line and leave the rest of the item blank.

Item 3. If you haven't filed a previous request for a fee waiver, fill in the date that you are filing this request on the first line.

If there was a previous order, check the second box and fill in the date you filed that request.

Item 4. Leave the rest of the first page, and all of the second page, blank.

Caption on Page 2. At the top of the page, fill in your present name and the name(s) of any other Petitioners. Leave the case number blank, as you don't have a case number yet.

You have now completed your part of the form. The court clerk will add other information, such as the case number, when you file your documents; the judge will complete the rest of the form.

When you receive the form back from the court, review it carefully, as your next steps depend on what it says.

- If box 4a is checked, your fee waiver process is complete and you can go ahead with your name change process.
- If box 4b is checked, pay particular attention to the deadlines in the additional boxes.
- If box 4b(1) is checked, this means the court has denied your request pending receiving more information from you. If you don't have any more information, you might have to go ahead and pay the filing fees. However, if the things that the court specifies in this item are things that you can provide, do so. This may mean filing a revised version of your Request to Waive Court Fees, with additional information included or

documents attached. If you have the information requested, ask the court clerk what is the best way to present it to the judge.

- If box 4b(2) is checked, this means the court has denied your request for specific reasons, which will be listed. Your choices at that point are to go ahead and pay the court fees, or to file a Request for Hearing About Court Fee Waiver Order (see instructions below). If you are going to ask for a hearing, you need to file the request within ten days after the date listed in the Clerk's Certificate of Service at the bottom of the order.

- If box 4c is checked, then the judge wants you to come to court and provide more information. The form should state what the judge wants to know and what documentation you should bring. Make sure that you go to court on the date specified.

Request for Hearing About Court Fee Waiver Order (Superior Court)

If the judge has denied your request for a fee waiver and you think the reasons given are incorrect, you can file this form to ask for a hearing in front of the judge.

CD-ROM

You'll find a blank copy of the Request for Hearing About Court Fee Waiver Order (Superior Court) on the CD-ROM at the back of the book. You can also download the form at www.courtinfo.ca.gov/forms/fillable/fw006.pdf.

Caption. On the right, fill in the address of the court, your case number, and, in the box for "Case Name," the words "Name Change Request of [your present name]."

Item 1. Fill in your present name and your address and telephone number.

Item 2. Fill in the words "In Pro Per."

Item 3. Fill in the date that is stamped in the upper right corner of the Order on Court Fee Waiver. Check the box below, and attach the Order.

Item 4. You do not need to do anything with this item.

Item 5. If you want to give the judge advance notice of what you're going to argue at the hearing, check this box and type in the statement you want to make about why the judge's decision was wrong. You should try very hard to contain everything you want to say in the space provided, but if it's just not possible, you can attach another page, following the instructions on the form. If there are documents you think the court should see and you didn't attach them to your original request, you can attach them to this form.

Date and signature line. Fill in the date, then print your present name on the left and sign on the right.

Take this form to the court and file it just as you did your original petition, along with the Order (see below). The clerk will give you a hearing date. See Chapter 9, "Appear in Court, if Necessary," for general information about preparing for a court hearing.

Order on Court Fee Waiver After Hearing

Along with your Request for Hearing, you must submit an Order to the court. The clerk won't file it, but will hold it in the file for the hearing.

CD-ROM

You'll find a blank copy of the Order on Court Fee Waiver After Hearing (Superior Court) on the CD-ROM at the back of the book. You can also download the form at www.courtinfo.ca.gov/forms/fillable/fw008.pdf.

Caption. On the right, fill in the address of the court, your case number, and, in the box for "Case Name," the words "Name Change Request of [your present name]."

Item 1. Fill in your present name and your address and telephone number.

Item 2. Fill in the words "In Pro Per."

Item 3. Fill in the date that is stamped in the upper right corner of your original request to waive court fees.

Item 4. Fill in the date of the hearing and the department where the hearing will be, if you know this information. If you don't, leave this blank and the clerk or judge will fill it in later. Check the box next to "Person in 1."

Item 5. Don't check any boxes; the judge will fill out this form. Do not date or sign the form.

Caption on Page 2. At the top of the page, fill in your present name and the name(s) of any other Petitioners, and the case number.

After the hearing, the judge's clerk will give you a completed Order that will tell you what to do—and whatever it says, that's what you'll have to do. You can't ask again for the judge to reconsider.

If the judge checked box 5a, your fee waiver has been granted and you can proceed with your case. If box 5b is checked, your request has been denied for the reasons stated on the Order. However, if box 5b(2) is checked, the court will allow you to pay the court fees over time, and will specify how much the payments are to be and what fees the payments apply to.

If the judge checked box 5c, your request has been partially granted and the Order will specify whether you must pay a certain percentage of all the fees, or only pay certain fees.

Arrange for Publication of the Order to Show Cause

State law requires a name change applicant to publish notice of the potential name change, in order to alert the public in case anyone wants to contest the action. You'll need to publish your Order to Show Cause in a local newspaper once a week for four weeks. So, your name change petition will give you the chance to get your name in the newspaper—at least, in the "Legal Notices" section, next to the want ads.

Almost any daily or weekly newspaper printed in your county is acceptable for publication, as long as the newspaper has been certified as a "newspaper of general circulation" by the superior court. If the paper runs legal ads—the ads in tiny print hidden away in some obscure section of the paper—then it's certified. Call the newspapers or check online and find out their rates for publishing an Order to Show Cause for Change of Name once a week for four weeks.

TIP

Weekly newspapers often charge lower fees. Often, free weekly newspapers are certified to publish legal notices, and their publication rates tend to be significantly lower than regular daily newspapers.

After you have filed your papers with the court, take a copy of your file-stamped and signed Order to Show Cause to the newspaper you have selected. Ask that the Order be published in the Legal Notices section once a week for four weeks, and pay the required fee. After the newspaper publishes the Order for all four weeks, it will prepare a form—called a Proof of Publication—in which it certifies that the Order was published. Ask the newspaper to send that statement directly to the court, with a copy to you. Give them your case number and caption information. You

should double-check that the newspaper sent the statement to the court by calling the newspaper a few days after the last publishing date.

In a few rural counties, where no newspaper is published, the court will order the clerk of the court to post the Order in three public places in the county. (Cal. Civ. Proc. Code § 1277.) If this is your situation, you'll need to have three extra file-stamped copies of the Order to Show Cause. Give these to the clerk and request the posting. Also ask the clerk to file a proof of posting in your case once the posting is complete.

SKIP AHEAD

If your name change petition does not involve a minor, you do not need to read the rest of this chapter. Skip ahead to Chapter 9 for instructions on finalizing your name change.

The Service of Process Requirement (Minor's Name Change)

You will need to complete service of process on another person only when you are filing a name change petition for a child. (Service of process is a legal term that means officially notifying an interested person of your court case.) You do this by giving that person certain legal papers, and only in the following circumstances:

- If the Petitioner is the child's parent and the child's other parent is alive but not filing with the Petitioner, the Petitioner must serve the other parent with the Order to Show Cause. (Cal. Civ. Proc. Code § 1277(a).)
- If the Petitioner is the child's legal guardian, the Petitioner needs to serve the child's living parent(s) or, if either or both parents have died or cannot be found, serve the child's grandparents, if living, with the Order to Show Cause. (Cal. Civ. Proc. Code § 1277(e).)

However, the Petitioner in either of the above circumstances can have the service of process requirement waived by the court if it is in the best interests of the child. (See "Waiver of Publication Requirement," below.)

TIP

Invite the other parent to join the petition, if possible. In most circumstances, the other parent has a legal right to contest the name change. Therefore we recommend that you start any name change process with a polite conversation with the other parent, rather than surprising the parent by serving legal papers. If the other parent agrees, you will not need to serve the papers—just fill them out and have the other parent sign them.

Of course, it may not be possible to get the other parent to agree to a child's name change, particularly when the other parent thinks it's a poor idea, is hostile,

or has essentially abandoned the child. In these instances, your best bet may be to serve the papers and hope the other parent doesn't show up—or that the court still approves the change as being in the best interests of the child.

CAUTION

Military parents have the right to object even after a name change is granted. If the other parent is in the military, he or she can contest a child's name change after it is granted if there was no opportunity to object at the time of the hearing due to his or her military service.

How to Serve the Order to Show Cause

As discussed above, you generally will be serving either a parent who hasn't joined your petition to change a minor's name or, in some cases, a grandparent. To make things simpler, we will refer to the person being served as "the other parent." How you will go about serving the Order to Show Cause depends on where the other parent lives:

- If you know where the other parent lives or works in California, you will need to serve the parent personally unless there is some reason that is impossible (like the other parent is avoiding service), in which case you will ask the court to allow you to publish notice or waive notice. (See

Choosing a Process Server

Neither you nor any other petitioner can serve papers on another person, because you are parties to the action. So you must pick someone else—this person is called the process server.

The person you choose must be at least 18 years old. The person can be a professional process server or a sheriff, marshal, or constable; in some circumstances, you could even have a friend or relative do it for you. If you are serving an out-of-state parent by certified mail, having a friend or relative do it will definitely be the least expensive and most convenient way.

If you need to make sure the other parent is served personally and you think it might be difficult, you should use a professional. You can find a professional process server in the yellow pages or on the Internet. Use common sense in choosing a process server: Make sure the person or company has experience and is licensed and/or bonded. If you want the sheriff to serve the papers, you can just call the sheriff's department. Professional process servers cost more, but they will probably act more quickly.

below for information on personal service and publication and waiver.)
- If the parent lives and works outside of California, you can serve the parent by certified mail, return receipt requested, or by personal service, as explained below.
- If you don't know where the other parent lives or works, or if you can't serve them personally for some reason, then you will have to resort to publication. Skip ahead to "Publishing Notice to the Other Parent," below, for instructions on publication.

Personal Service (California or Elsewhere)

You must make an effort to serve the other parent personally with the Order to Show Cause. If the other parent will cooperate, you can simply arrange to have someone drop off the papers at a time that is convenient, and then have that person sign the Proof of Service. (See "Completing the Proof of Service Form," below.) Otherwise, you will have to ask someone to track the other parent down and serve them, as described below. This means that the server must personally hand the parent the Order to Show Cause and the Petition.

Give the server the following:
- the name of the other parent
- a photo or a physical description
- information about where the server can find the other parent—at home or at work or both (be as detailed as you can), and
- a copy of the Petition and the Order to Show Cause.

If you are using a professional process server—or a county sheriff, marshal, or constable—this person will know the routine. Call ahead to find out exactly what the server needs from you.

If you decide to have a friend or relative make service, tell this person to announce to the other parent, "I have court papers for you." Then the person should hand the papers to the parent. That's it. Once the parent takes the papers, the server can walk away. If the parent won't open the door, turns and runs, or in any other way tries to avoid service, the server can just drop the papers and leave. Service will still be completed.

If the other parent isn't home, but someone else answers the door, tell your server to keep trying. If your server tries to personally serve the parent at least three times, and the parent is not available any of those times, the server can leave a copy of the notice with another person at the location. This is called substituted service. In this situation, the server must leave the papers with someone who appears to be in a position to get the papers to the absent parent (in other words, not someone who appears to be passing through or to have no authority to deliver papers). If the notice is left at home, it must be left with someone who is competent to receive it, which means someone over the age of 18. The server should ask for the name of the person who took the papers, so that it can be included on the proof of service form.

If your server uses substituted service, the server must also mail another copy of the paperwork (by regular mail) to the place where the first copy was left.

Once service is effective (for regular personal service, it is effective when the person receives the documents in hand; for substituted service, it is effective on the tenth day after mailing), have the server fill out the Proof of Service, as described below. Then you can file the proof of service with the clerk. Be sure to get back from the clerk at least one file-stamped copy for your records.

Service by Certified or Registered Mail (Outside California Only)

If the parent is out of state and will receive a certified letter, then service by certified mail, with a return receipt requested, is appropriate. (You can't use certified mail if the absent parent is in California.)

It's not wise to use this type of service if you know only the person's work address, because it will be difficult for you to ensure that the parent and not someone else at the work address signs for the mail. In that case you should try to have someone serve the other parent personally.

Make sure the server indicates "deliver to addressee only" on the post office form. The return receipt should come back to the process server. When it does, the server should attach it to a completed proof of service form. (See below.)

Service is effective on the tenth calendar day after mailing. Once service is effective, file the Proof of Service with the clerk. Be sure to get back from the clerk at least one file-stamped copy of each document for your records.

If the parent won't sign for the mail, then this form of service has failed. You will have to serve the parent by personal service or, if that doesn't work, by publication. (See below for more about publication.)

Completing the Proof of Service Form

Regardless of which method you use, you will have to obtain a form called a Proof of Service, which is a sworn statement that proves the required steps were actually carried out to serve the notice on the parent. The server signs and dates the Proof of Service form, and you file it with the county clerk as soon as service is effective.

If the server personally served the other parent in California, the server can simply sign the Proof of Service form and give it to you.

If the server personally served the other parent out of state, the Proof of Service form must be made by a sworn and notarized affidavit (this is a good reason to use a professional server for serving parents who are outside of California). The server should complete the Proof of Service form, attach the required affidavit to it, and send both documents back to you.

CD-ROM

There is a special Proof of Service form for the Order to Show Cause for a name change, form NC-121. You can find a blank copy on the CD-ROM at the back of the book, or you can download it from the judicial council website at www.courtinfo.ca.gov/forms/fillable/nc121.pdf.

Either you or the server can fill out the form, but only the server can sign it. To complete the Proof of Service form, follow these instructions:

Caption. Type your name and address, the name of the court, and the case number in the appropriate boxes. Check the appropriate box depending on whether service was personal or by mail.

Item 1. You don't need to do anything with this item.

Item 2. Put the server's home or business address.

Item 3a. If you used personal service, whether in California or outside of California, check the box under item 3a and fill in the information requested under items (1) through (4). If the server substituted service on someone other than the parent, under item (1) type in the name of the person served and immediately following their name type in "substituted for [name of other parent]; see attached declaration." Then attach a declaration describing the efforts made to serve the other parent. (See below for information on how to do a declaration.)

Item 3b. If you used mail service on someone outside of California, check this box and fill in the information requested in items (2)(a) through (2)(d).

Reminder. If service was made outside California, attach the professional server's affidavit of service.

Have the server sign and date the form. File it in the same place where you filed your petition. Be sure to get back several file-stamped copies for your records.

Publishing Notice to the Other Parent

Even when you can't find the other parent, you must still give notice of the name change Petition. You also might give notice this way if the other parent is avoiding service. In these circumstances the law allows you to meet the service requirement by publishing the Order to Show Cause in the county where the other parent last lived. You've already made arrangements to publish your Order to Show Cause in the county where you filed your Petition, so you're an old hand at this.

If the other parent's last known address was in the same county where your Petition is filed, you will not need to publish notice again. If this is the case, skip ahead to "Waiver of Publication Requirement," below, for information on getting a waiver of the publication requirement. However, if the other parent's last known address was in a different county from the one where you published your Order to Show Cause, you will have to publish again in that county.

Before you can publish the Order to Show Cause as a means of giving notice, you must do the following:

- make a sincere, concerted effort to find the other parent
- demonstrate to the court your efforts to find the parent, and ask the court to authorize service by publication
- get a signed order from a judge authorizing you to publish, and
- publish the Order to Show Cause in an approved newspaper at least once a week for four weeks in a row and prove to the court that the citation was published.

All of these steps are described in detail below.

Try to Find the Other Parent

Before a court will allow you to notify the missing parent of the hearing by publication, you must show that you unsuccessfully searched for the parent.

SKIP AHEAD

If you know the address of the other parent but are publishing notice because you can't make service in any of the ways discussed in above, you can skip ahead to "Waiver of Publication Requirement," below.

Ways to Search for the Other Parent

You may be wondering how hard you must work to find the other parent—must you hire Scotland Yard to search the world, or

Military Location Services

The steps you take to locate an absent parent in the military will depend on the branch. We provide a summary below. Be aware that, with current fears about terrorism, the rules are in flux. If these methods lead to a dead end, seek assistance from the court clerk.

Navy. The Navy's locator service helps locate individuals on active duty and those whose service ended less than a year ago. In addition, the Navy will forward letters as long as you put the correct postage on the envelope. Unless you are in the military, or are a family member of someone who is, the fee for researching an address is $3.50 per address. Mail your correspondence, with check or money order payable to the United States Treasurer, to the following address: World Wide Locator, Bureau of Naval Personnel, PERS 312F, 5720 Integrity Drive, Millington, TN 38055-3120. You can also call the locator service at 901-874-5111.

Air Force. The Air Force locator service will forward mail as long as the correct postage is on the envelope and any required fee has been paid. You can also request addresses by mail, for a fee of $3.50 per address if you are in the military yourself, or $5.20 per address if you are not. Mail your correspondence with your fee, check, or money order payable to the United States Treasurer, to the following address: Headquarters AFMPC/RMIQL, 550 C Street West, Suite 50, Randolph Air Force Base, TX, 78150-4752, 210-565-2660.

Army. If you are not in the military and are not a current family member of the person you are searching for, the only way to locate someone in the Army is to go through the Red Cross locator. Red Cross chapters are listed in local telephone books and on the American Red Cross website at www.redcross.org/where/where .html. As of the writing of this book, the Army had suspended its own locator service. If you want to contact the Army, use this address: Commander, U.S. Army Enlisted Records & Evaluation Center, ATTN: Locator, 8899 East 56th Street, Fort Benjamin Harrison, IN 46249-5301.

Marines. For information on locating someone who is in the Marines, write to the following address: Headquarters, U.S. Marine Corps, Personnel Management Support Branch (MMSB-17), 2008 Elliot Road, Quantico, VA 22134, 703-696-6762.

Coast Guard. You can make a request via email at csutton@comdt.uscg.mil. Or send a written request to the following address: Coast Guard Personnel Command (CGPC - adm-3), 2100 Second St, SW, Washington, DC 20593-0001. Also see www.uscg.mil/locator.

There are also a few online sources for locating military personnel:

- www.einvestigator.com/links/military_locator.htm
- www.defense.gov/lending/questions.aspx
- www.afpc.randolph.af.mil/library/airforcelocator.asp

will a quick search through the local phone book suffice? The answer is somewhere in between. The following search techniques are taken in part from the search criteria issued by the Los Angeles County Superior Court. Your county may have its own search criteria. Check with the clerk to find out. Generally speaking, you will need to follow at least these steps before a court will allow you to notify the absent parent by publication:

- Find the last known address of the other parent. You will have to tell the court how, when, and from whom you obtained the address.

- Check at the other parent's last known address. If the people living there have no information about where you can find the parent, ask the neighbors on the right and left. You can do this either by letter, by walking through the neighborhood yourself, or by sending an investigator to the neighborhood.

- If the last known address is a mental or penal institution, contact the person in charge of the institution, ask for current address information from its records, and then contact that address.

- Ask all known relatives, friends, former employers, and other people likely to know where the parent is. You must tell the court their names and what relationship they are to the parent. Give dates and results of your inquiries.

- Some counties require that you submit a declaration about whether the other parent is in the military. Check with your county clerk to see whether your county requires that you contact the military services to see if you can find the parent that way. The military has become much more closed-mouthed about the location of service personnel since the terrorist attacks on September 11, 2001, and you may have a difficult time getting any information. See "Military Location Services," above.

- Contact the tax assessor's office in the county of the parent's last known address. Ask for current information. You can probably do this by phone. Check with the county clerk to find out whether phone verification is acceptable to the court or whether a written certificate of search is required.

- Search the Internet by putting the person's name into a search engine such as Google or Bing. There are also Internet services that you can use to locate people for a small fee; this is a good thing to do if you can afford it, because it will show the court that you have really tried hard to find the absent parent.

- Follow up any other lead you can think of, including contacts with unions, trade associations, or licensing agencies that may have information.

⚠ CAUTION

You do not have to check the DMV or voter registration. If a judge or clerk tells you to search the department of motor vehicles or voter registration before an order for publication will be issued, you should tactfully tell the judge or clerk that the law now prohibits the court from requiring you to do these searches. (Code of Civil Procedure § 415.50(e).)

Log Your Attempts

When you try to find the other parent, keep records of your activities using the Missing Parent Search Log on the CD-ROM. A filled-out sample is shown below. You'll see that there are lines for entering the date of each attempt, the place of the attempt, the person attempting to find the parent, and the result. You'll need this information in order to convince a judge that service by publication is appropriate, and it will be helpful to have all of your notes in one place.

Sample Missing Parent Search Log

Date search initiated	Person performing the search	Person or entity contacted	Contact information	Results
May 2, 20xx	Miriam Chow, family friend	Last known address—checked with neighbors and current residents	123 State Street, Anywhere, CA	Talked to neighbors on right and left of house (119, 121, and 127). They were unaware of parent's current address.
May 4, 20xx	Me	Tax Assessor	200 Main Street	No records of home ownership in this county
May 5, 20xx	Me	Google search		No hits for parent's name

Write Declarations
Describing Your Attempts

Whoever conducts the search will eventually need to sign something called a declaration, describing the attempts and results. If you had someone help you, so that both of you did some of the work of trying to find the missing parent, then each of you will have to sign a separate declaration. (A declaration is simply a document in which people swear that what they have said is true to the best of their knowledge. You can't swear to something that someone else did, so each person must sign their own declaration. For guidance on creating a declaration that you can present to the court, see "Creating a Declaration," below.)

Attach the declaration(s) to the application when you ask the court to order publication. (See below for more about seeking a court order.) If you made an inquiry by mail about the whereabouts of the parent, attach any returned correspondence or evidence of mailing.

Creating a Declaration

A declaration is the written testimony of a witness. In a declaration, the witness lists pertinent facts and then swears that they are true to the best of the witness's knowledge. A declaration is always written in the first person, from the witness's point of view. (If you are the one drafting the declaration and someone else is signing it, you'll write it from their point of view.)

You can use a Judicial Council form, MC-030, to create all of the declarations mentioned in this book. You'll find a blank copy of that form on the CD-ROM at the back of the book. You can also download it from the judicial council website at www.courtinfo.ca.gov/forms/fillable/mc030.pdf or fill it out online.

The first sentence of your declaration should always say that the witness is an adult, and it should state whether the witness is a party to the action. (You and the other parent are both parties.) Use the first person pronoun "I." For example: "I, John Smith, am an adult resident of San Mateo County, and am the petitioner in this case."

Declarations are written in numbered paragraphs—one fact per paragraph. Even if you need a declaration from someone other than yourself, you should be the one to write the declaration, putting in the facts that you think are important. Then have the witness read it and sign it. If the witness wants to change something you've written, that's fine. The witness can simply cross through the incorrect information and handwrite (legibly in blue or black ink) the correct information. Have the witness initial each change.

Choose a Newspaper for Publication

Your Order to Show Cause will need to appear in the newspaper of general circulation in California that is most likely to give notice of the hearing to the other parent. Select a daily newspaper in the area where the parent was last known to reside, just as you did in your county. If the parent never lived in California, or if the parent's last known residence was in another state, you do not have an obligation to publish in a newspaper in the state where the parent was last known to reside. In that situation, you should be able to get the court to waive the publication requirement. (See "Waiver of Publication Requirement," below.)

Prepare Documents

You will need to prepare two documents: an Application and Declaration and an Order for Publication. Some counties have standard forms for these documents, so ask your county clerk for them. If they don't have standard forms, use the forms we provide. We include samples in this chapter (but these forms are not included on the CD-ROM, because they're too specific to each individual situation. You can use the pleading paper that is on the CD-ROM to write your own forms.).

Application and Declaration

To convince the court to allow you to give notice by publication, you'll file a document called an Application and Declaration. This document contains the evidence that the court will review to determine whether publication is appropriate. Thus, you should be extremely detailed about your attempts to locate the other parent, which won't be difficult if you have dutifully filled out your Missing Parent Search Log.

In this document, you do the following:

- give your name, the child's name, and the absent parent's name
- describe your unsuccessful efforts at locating the other parent or the server's unsuccessful attempts at serving the parent
- describe any documents that you are attaching to the application
- request that the court issue an order directing publication of the Order to Show Cause in your chosen newspaper once a week for four consecutive weeks, and
- swear under penalty of perjury that everything you've written is true to the best of your knowledge.

If you know the address of the parent but are publishing notice because you weren't able to serve the parent personally, explain in the application that service could not be made except by publication. Tell the court in detail why the parent could not be served. Describe each attempt that was made and why it failed, and

Formatting Court Documents

When it comes to court documents, appearances count. All California courts require that documents you file with them look a certain way. (These rules are in Rule 201 of the California Rules of Court for Superior Courts.) Follow these guidelines when formatting your court papers:

- Type the document on 8½ × 11 numbered legal paper, called pleading paper. (You can usually buy pleading paper from a stationery store, or you can use the sheet that is on the CD-ROM.)
- Type your name, address, phone number, and "Petitioner In Pro Per" in the extreme upper left.
- Type Superior Court of California on line 8 and County of [Your County] on line 9.

- Type your first, middle, and last name (do not use initials) underneath the county name on the left-hand side of the page.
- Type the case number and the title of the document underneath the county name on the right-hand side of the page.
- Start typing the body of the document on line 13.
- In a footer between the 28th line and the bottom edge of the page (below the page number), type the document's name.
- Whenever you handwrite something on a document—including your signature—use only blue or black ink.

The Nolo forms we provide for you in this book are formatted correctly, so if you copy them, you should be fine. You do not need to worry about formatting Judicial Council forms—they are already in the proper format.

attach a declaration of the person who tried to serve the parent.

Attach any documents that you gathered in the course of your search—for example, printouts from Internet searches showing that there was no result, a receipt from the tax assessor showing that the person is not listed, or an envelope that came back because the person is no longer at the last known address. Keep a copy of each for your records.

CAUTION

Personal service is required if you find out where the other parent lives. If you learn the other parent's address at any time during the process of asking the court for permission to publish notice, you will have to stop that process and try to serve the parent personally, as described above. Only if those efforts are unsuccessful can you then ask the court again for permission to serve by publication.

Sample Application and Declaration—Publication of Citation

1 Joe Jake Nolo
2 555 Self-Help Drive
   Berkeley, CA 94611
3 510-555-1111
   In Pro Per
4

5

6
                    SUPERIOR COURT OF CALIFORNIA
7   COUNTY OF ALAMEDA

8   In the Petition of   )   NO. 1212
9   JOE JAKE NOLO,   )
       For Change of Name   )   APPLICATION AND
10   )   DECLARATION—PUBLICATION
)   OF ORDER TO SHOW CAUSE
11   _____)

12
       Application is hereby made for an order directing service of the
13 Order to Show Cause in this proceeding on Mary Smith (referred to as
14 "the other parent") by publication in The San Francisco Chronicle,
    which is a newspaper of general circulation in this state most likely
15 to give the absent parent notice of this proceeding. In support of this
16 application, I, Joe Nolo, declare:
17   I am the party requesting a name change for a minor. I am the minor's
18 father; Mary Smith is the minor's mother.
       I do not know where Mary Smith lives. I made the following attempts
19 to locate her:
20   Mary Smith's last known address was 222 State Street, San Francisco,
21 CA 94114. On February 12, 20xx, I inquired at the above address and
    learned from the current resident that the other parent no longer lives
22 there. The current resident does not know the whereabouts of the other
23 parent. I inquired with neighbors to the right and left of the address,
24 and they did not know the other parent's current address or where she
25 works.
       I made the following additional efforts to locate the other parent
26 through relatives, friends, and others likely to know her whereabouts.
27 The only persons likely to know the whereabouts of the other parent are
28 shown below:

1 John Smith, brother.
   Address: 12 E. Street, Anywhere, California.

2 Date of Inquiry: Feb. 10, 20xx.

3 Mabel Smith, mother.
   Address: 43 Clover Drive, Anywhere, California.

4 Date of Inquiry: Feb. 15, 20xx.

5 James Duncan, friend.
   Address: 123 Oak Street, Anywhere, California.

6 Date of Inquiry: Feb. 20, 20xx.

7 ABC Construction Co., former employer.
   Address: 567 North Street, Anywhere, California.

8 Date of Inquiry: Feb. 24, 20xx.

9

10 The people listed above either did not know the other parent's

11 whereabouts or did not respond to my inquiries.

12 On March 1, 20xx, I inquired of the other parent's union, Local 1203,

13 as to her whereabouts. The union has no record that she is a current

    member of its union.

14 On March 2, 20xx, I searched the San Francisco County Tax Assessor's

15 records, but found no records of the whereabouts of the other parent.

16 On March 2, 20xx, I conducted an Internet search by putting the

17 other parent's full name into the "Google" search engine. No records

18 were found relating to the absent parent. I also used the "Yahoo" search

19 engine "people search" function and found no records relating to the

20 other parent. Printouts of the search results are attached hereto.

21 WHEREFORE, Petitioner asks that the court issue its order directing

22 service of the Order to Show Cause for Change of Name on Mary Smith

    by publication in The San Francisco Chronicle once a week for four

23 successive weeks as provided in Section 6064 of the Government Code.

24 I declare under penalty of perjury that the foregoing is true and

25 correct and that this declaration was executed on June 12, 20xx at

26 Berkeley, California.

27 Dated: June 12, 20xx

28 _Joe Jake Nolo_

Order for Publication

Next, prepare an order for the court to sign. The judge will sign it upon approving your application. A sample is shown below.

Sample Order for Publication of Citation

1	Joe Jake Nolo
2	555 Self-Help Drive
	Berkeley, CA 94611
3	510-555-1111
	In Pro Per
4	

```
 1   Joe Jake Nolo
 2   555 Self-Help Drive
     Berkeley, CA 94611
 3   510-555-1111
     In Pro Per
 4

 5

 6                       SUPERIOR COURT OF CALIFORNIA
 7                           COUNTY OF ALAMEDA

 8   Petition of              )        No. 1212
 9   JOE JAKE NOLO,           )
     For Change of Name       )        ORDER FOR PUBLICATION
10   _____)      OF ORDER TO SHOW CAUSE
11

12       On reading the declaration of Joe Nolo on file herein and it

13   satisfactorily appearing to me that the residence of Mary Smith, the

14   mother of the minor who is the subject of the name change petition filed

15   herein, is unknown to Petitioner,

16       IT IS ORDERED that service of the Order to Show Cause in this matter

17   be made on Mary Smith by publication in the San Francisco Chronicle,

18   which is hereby designated as the newspaper most likely to give notice

19   to Mary Smith. Publication is to be made at least once each week for four

20   successive weeks.

21       IT IS FURTHER ORDERED that a copy of the Order to Show Cause for

22   Change of Name be forthwith mailed to Mary Smith if Mary Smith's

23   address is ascertained before the expiration of the time prescribed for

24   publication of the citation.

25

26       Dated: _____

27                            _____
                                    Judge of the Superior Court
28
```

Get Your Order for Publication Signed

Next, take your application and order to the county clerk. Bring originals and three copies. First, go to the main county clerk and ask where the presiding judge sits. Then, ask the clerk of the presiding judge when you can get the Order for Publication signed. The clerk may take the documents from you and not require that you see the judge, or the judge may wish to talk to you personally. The clerk might ask you to leave your paperwork for signature and come back later that day—or even the following day—to pick it up. If you don't want to come back and would prefer to have your signed Order mailed to you, attach a stamped, self-addressed envelope to your papers. Make sure you leave enough copies for you to receive file-stamped copies back.

If you live in a large, busy county, you may not get to deliver your papers to the presiding judge's clerk—instead, you'll very likely be required to leave them with the main clerk along with a prepaid envelope for return of the documents to you.

> **CAUTION**
> **Don't spend more than 90 days from the start of your search to the date you submit your publication paperwork to the judge.** Otherwise, the judge may decide that your search is obsolete, and you'll have to start all over again.

Arrange for Publication

Just as you did to publish in the county where you filed your Petition, give the selected newspaper a copy of the Order to Show Cause. The Order to Show Cause must be published at least once each week for four weeks in a row. Service is complete seven days after the date of the fourth and last publication (about four weeks after the date of first publication). After service by publication is complete, there must be at least another ten days before the hearing date (check your local county rules for the exact number of days). This is called the additional notice period. If the additional notice period is ten days, you must make sure the first publication date is at least 40 days before the hearing date. Obviously, it's important that you not delay in publishing the Order to Show Cause after you get your order. Tell the newspaper to publish immediately, and inform the newspaper of when service must be complete.

After the newspaper publishes the Order for all four weeks, it will prepare a form—called a Proof of Publication—in which it certifies that the Order was published. Ask the newspaper to send that statement directly to the court, with a copy to you. You should double-check that the newspaper sent the statement to the court by calling the newspaper a few days after the last publishing date.

Waiver of Publication Requirement

Under some circumstances, you can ask the court to dispense with (waive) the requirement to notify the other parent of your child's name change. To get the court to agree, you'll have to explain exactly why you believe service is not necessary. Some situations in which publication can be waived are:

- when you can't find the other parent, and the other parent's last known address is in the same county as the one where you filed your petition (so that your legal notice is sufficient)
- when you can't find the other parent, and the other parent's last known address is outside of California
- when you don't know the identity of the other parent (as where you are unaware of the identity of the child's father)
- when the other parent has not contacted the child for a significant period of time, and
- when you find that the other parent is impossible to serve personally or by certified mail (if outside of California).

To apply for a waiver, prepare an Application and Order Dispensing With Notice. A sample is shown below. This document is both your formal request to the court to waive notice and, if the judge agrees and signs the paper, the court's official order waiving notice. In this form, your job is to explain concisely and persuasively why the court should not require you to notify the other parent. To succeed, you must convince the court that service would be impossible or useless. Waiver will not be approved where service is simply inconvenient. Here is some sample language you can use or modify in the sample below:

- [Child]'s father is unknown. He is not listed on [Child]'s birth certificate, a copy of which is attached to this document and incorporated herein.
- [Child]'s mother's whereabouts are unknown. Her last known address was 222 Cedar Street in Oakland, Alameda County. The Order to Show Cause in this case has already been published in Alameda County in connection with the Name Change Petition, and there would be no point in duplicating publication in the same county.
- [Child]'s father and I were divorced on [date], and I do not know his whereabouts. He was denied visitation rights with [Child] on the basis of prior abuse and neglect, and he has had no contact with [Child] since then. A copy of the divorce decree and custody order is attached to this document and incorporated herein.
- [Child]'s father has had no contact with [Child] since [specify date], and has not made child support payments since [specify date]. I have remarried,

and [Child] is known by the last name of my husband, [specify name]. My husband has acted as a father to [Child] since [specify date]. (The period between your request and the last date on which the other parent had contact with the child must be a significant period of time to have publication waived on these grounds—a year or two is probably not enough.)

If you want to have the notice requirement waived because you cannot locate the other parent, you should also file a declaration with your application stating the efforts that you made to find the absent parent, such as we described in "Try to Find the Other Parent," above. If you decide to file a declaration, tell the court in your Application and Order Dispensing With Notice that you are doing so. Below,

you'll find a sample Application and Order Dispensing With Notice.

Use the sample below as a guide and type yours on copies of the pleading paper that's provided on the CD-ROM at the back of the book. Be sure to complete the forms and file them according to the requirements laid out in your county's local rules.

If the court grants your application, then you have completed your service requirement and you can go ahead and finalize the child's name change. See Chapter 9 for instructions on how to do that.

If the court denies your application for waiver, the judge will give you instructions about what you need to do next. Most likely you will need to publish notice, as described above.

Sample Application and Order Dispensing With Notice

1	Joe Jake Nolo
2	555 Self-Help Drive
	Berkeley, CA 94611
3	510-555-1111
	In Pro Per
4	
5	
6	
7	SUPERIOR COURT OF CALIFORNIA
	COUNTY OF ALAMEDA
8	
9	In the Petition of) NO. 1212
	JOE JAKE NOLO,)
	For Change of Name) APPLICATION AND ORDER
10	) DISPENSING WITH NOTICE
	) RE: CHANGE OF NAME
11	_____)

Application is hereby made for an order dispensing with notice
to Mary Smith, the mother of the minor Applicant in this name
change proceeding. The whereabouts of Mary Smith are unknown to the
Petitioner. Attempts to locate Mary Smith are set out in detail in the
declaration(s) filed in support of this application. *[replace with other
reasons or add information as appropriate]* Petitioner requests that the
court issue an order dispensing with notice to Mary Smith.

Dated: _____

_____
Your name

IT IS THE ORDER OF THIS COURT that notice to Mary Smith, the mother
of the minor Applicant, be dispensed with.

Dated: _____

_____
Judge of the Superior Court

Final Steps Toward Changing Your Name

Appear in Court, if Necessary

For the final step in your name change petition, you may need to appear briefly in court at a hearing on your Petition for Change of Name. This is usually a very simple proceeding. Often, in fact, the court will not hold a hearing at all.

Find Out Whether or Not the Court Will Hold a Hearing

If all your paperwork is in order and there is no opposition, the court may grant your name change without holding a hearing. (Cal. Civ. Proc. Code § 1278.) (In some counties, courts may require a hearing even if there is no objection.)

To find out whether you will need to appear, call the court clerk a day or two before the scheduled hearing date that is listed on your Order to Show Cause. Explain that you have filed a name change petition and give the clerk your case number and scheduled hearing date. Ask the clerk:

- whether any written objections have been filed (in 99% of cases the answer will be no), and
- whether the court will be holding a hearing.

If the answer to the second question is no, and the court intends to grant the name change based on the papers, without a hearing, the clerk will tell you when and where to pick up your signed Decree Changing Name.

SKIP AHEAD

If you learn from the court clerk that you do not need to appear in court, skip ahead to "Steps to Take After Your Name Change."

Prepare to Attend the Hearing If Required

If you have to appear in court, make sure you know where and when the hearing will be held. Bring with you:

- Copies of all the documents you've filed, as well as a copy of the Proof of Publication, if the newspaper sent you a copy. Although the judge will have the originals, it's a good idea to bring along copies just in case.
- Several extra copies of the Decree Changing Name form.
- Copies of any final divorce decree and other relevant documents relating to support or visitation, for those petitioning to change a child's name without the consent of the other parent. Also prepare and bring a written record showing the dates of the other parent's support payments and visits to the child. Again, as discussed in Chapter 4, a court is more likely to find that a proposed name change is in the best interests of a child if the other parent has not supported or visited the child.

If you can't make the scheduled court hearing, you may be able to arrange for a "continuance"—a rescheduling—by contacting the court clerk. Courts have different procedures for arranging continuances. For example, you may need to send a letter to the court confirming the new date. Also, if anyone has filed an objection to your petition, you'll need to notify that person formally of your request for a continuance.

Attend the Court Hearing

On the day of the court hearing, plan to arrive at the courthouse at least half an hour before your scheduled hearing. Courtrooms are often called "departments."

You may already know what department your case is in—sometimes the clerk puts that information on the Order to Show Cause when you file it. If not, then to find out which courtroom or department you need to go to, look for a posted list outside or just inside the clerk's office—each case on the schedule for that day will be listed under a certain department or courtroom. Your court may use a master calendar system whereby lots of cases are assigned to one big courtroom and then are assigned to other judges from there. If you are confused, ask the court clerk for help.

Once you've found the correct room, it's good to let the courtroom clerk (sitting in front of or next to the judge) know that you are there. There will be other cases scheduled for the same time as yours, so don't worry if you are not called right away. You can check with the clerk or bailiff or perhaps on a bulletin board to find out where you are placed on the schedule.

TIP

If you're concerned about privacy for your gender change, you can ask to go last. When you check in with the clerk, ask to be put at the end of the calendar—you're less likely to have an audience that way.

Once you are sure you are in the right place, sit down and watch the cases ahead of you, so you get a feel for the procedure. Above all, don't be intimidated if there are lawyers milling around. You should have no problem handling this hearing on your own.

If you are petitioning on behalf of a child, state law does not require you to bring the child to the hearing. However, your court's local rules may require the child to attend, so you should check these rules to be sure. (See Chapter 8.) Either way, it is usually best to bring the child, especially if the child is old enough to have an opinion about the name change.

Uncontested Case

Again, most courts do not require a court appearance unless objections were filed to the proposed name change. But local rules vary, and sometimes judges want to consider the name change in court even if no one has objected. Bear in mind that the judge must grant your request unless there is a good reason for denial, so you will normally just state your request with no need to convince the judge of anything.

Here's how a court hearing will normally work.

You will be sitting in the courtroom, listening to other cases, when finally the bailiff calls the number and name of your case. For example, you may hear, "Case Number 01-3413, In re Coughlin" or "Application of Coughlin." Rise and step forward past the low fence or wall that separates the spectators' section of the courtroom from the judge's area.

The courtroom clerk may ask you to take the witness stand or may direct you to a table or podium facing the judge. You will be sworn in or, if you wish, affirmed ("to tell the truth," and so on). You may be asked to "stipulate" (agree) to having your case heard by a commissioner instead of a judge. For purposes of a name change, a commissioner has the same authority as a judge, and you should sign the stipulation.

Call the judge or commissioner "Your Honor." The judge or commissioner will normally ask you a few questions to become better informed about your petition. For example, "Ms. Coughlin, you have petitioned this court to change your last name to Peters. You state that you are already going by this name. How long have you done so? Why have you begun to use this name?"

Answer the judge's questions briefly. For example, "Yes, Your Honor, I have been using the name Peters for three years," or, "Your Honor, after I divorced my former husband, I planned to continue to use his last name. But, later I wanted to use a different last name. I decided to go by Peters," or, "Your Honor, Peters is the family name of my maternal grandmother. I was close with her as a child, and I decided I would like to honor her and feel close to my heritage by using her name."

TIP

Ask for help if you need it and ask for a continuance if you have a problem. Judges are generally helpful to people acting as their own attorneys for name changes. Feel free to ask the judge or commissioner to explain any questions you don't understand. And in the unusual event that the judge is not helpful or is asking you questions you think are inappropriate (much more likely in a gender-change case than a standard name change), you can ask for a continuance (delay) so that you can consult a lawyer about what to do.

Once satisfied that the name change should be allowed, the judge will say something like "Granted" or "So ordered" and will sign the Decree Changing Name. You say, "Thank you, Your Honor" and step down.

Contested Case

If anyone files written objections to your name change, you'll definitely need to appear in court. You should receive a copy of the written objections at the mailing address you put on your petition. If you don't receive an objection, but suspect one is likely to be made, go to the clerk's office and ask to see your file. If an objection is on file, you can get a copy for a small fee.

Anyone who files a written opposition to your petition must state a specific reason for the objection. Most objections are for one of the reasons listed below:

- A relative does not approve of a minor's proposed name change. For example, a natural father may not want his child's name changed to the stepparent's last name or mother's birth name.
- A prominent person with a name similar to your proposed name claims you intend to impersonate him or her or otherwise capitalize on the name.
- A creditor suspects you want to change your name to try to avoid paying your debts.

If you face a contested hearing, you may wish to arrange for a lawyer to represent you. If so, you'll probably want to emphasize that you've already done all the paperwork and simply want to be represented at the hearing. This shouldn't involve more than a few hours of work, so the fee should be modest. (See Chapter 11.)

However, you should also consider representing yourself, especially if the written objection isn't substantial and can easily be countered. For example, if someone with a name similar to your new name objects, claiming you want to impersonate her or steal her identity, you will need to tell the judge your legitimate reason for the change. This is not complicated. Just be prepared to explain

how you decided on the name—maybe it was your uncle's name or your sister has called you by this nickname since birth. Perhaps the name you've chosen is similar to the objector's name only by coincidence.

A contested case proceeds pretty much the same way as an uncontested case. You will be sworn in to tell the truth. The court may ask you to testify from the witness stand, as if you were a witness at a regular trial. The judge will give you a chance to state your reasons for the name change. The judge may help you do this by asking pertinent questions, or may simply ask you to proceed. To deal with the possibility that the judge may not be particularly helpful, you'll want to be prepared to make a short statement about the key reasons that your proposed name change should be approved. In some situations, after you have finished, the court will call on the person opposing the name change to voice her objections. After this is done, you'll normally have a chance to reply.

Let's take a look at a couple of examples to see how the process works. Kristophos Yukabonkerz-Kapowpolis (we'll call him "Kris") files a petition to change his name to Kris Kapow. Unfortunately for Kris, two written objections are filed, one by Cruz Creditor, to whom Kris owes $3,000, and another by Chris Capow, a famous Hollywood stuntwoman who specializes in being shot out of cannons. Cruz thinks Kris wants to use his new name to avoid repaying his debt, and Chris is afraid Kris will try to profit from his similar-sounding new name. Here's what Kris says upon being sworn in and taking the witness stand:

> *"Good morning, Your Honor. I currently use the name Kris Kapow, and I am petitioning the court to approve my use of this new name, from my former name, Kristophos Yukabonkerz-Kapowpolis. I want to change my name because my present last name is obviously very difficult to pronounce and spell. And because it just plain won't fit on the back of my uniform. I am a college football player and hope to turn pro next year. I do not propose this new name in order to avoid any debts, including the one to Mr. Creditor. I am fully aware that a name change has no legal effect on this or any other debt and am willing to make this clear in writing to Mr. Creditor.*
>
> *"As to Ms. Capow's objection, I do not intend to use my new last name to profit from her identical-sounding last name. In fact, before she filed her objection, I had never heard of her. My own occupation as a football player is quite different from hers. I chose the new name "Kapow" because that word is contained in my much longer birth name. Out of pride in my ethnic heritage, I wish to retain a small part of that name."*

Hannah Morton has petitioned to change her young daughter Cynthia's last name from Davis to Morton. Hannah's ex-husband and Cynthia's father, John Davis, has not contacted either Hannah or Cynthia for the last 18 months—since Cynthia was two. After Hannah served

John with the Order to Show Cause in this case, John filed an objection with the court. He says that he is still Cynthia's father, so she should bear his name. He claims that he has been out of work for more than a year, so he couldn't make child support payments and was embarrassed to contact his daughter. Here is what Hannah says to the court:

> *"Good morning, Your Honor. My name is Hannah Morton. I am the mother of Cynthia Davis, and I am petitioning the court to change Cynthia's name to Cynthia Morton. Currently, Cynthia bears the family name of her father, John Davis. Mr. Davis and I were married when Cynthia was born, but we were divorced two years later. In the divorce decree, I was given full custody of Cynthia because the court found that I could provide Cynthia with a more stable and nurturing environment than Mr. Davis could. The court granted Mr. Davis visitation of two weekends per month with his daughter, and the court ordered Mr. Davis to pay me $1,000 per month for Cynthia's care. I have filed a copy of the divorce order in this case, and I also have a copy here if the court needs it.*
>
> *"Mr. Davis made his required payments for six months. During that time, he visited Cynthia about once per month and each visit was only for a few hours, rather than an entire weekend. After those six months, Mr. Davis stopped contacting us and did not send any more child support payments. I tried to call him but he did not return my calls. Since that time, I have had to take a second job to support myself and Cynthia. It has been hard, but I have still provided*

Cynthia with a loving and nurturing environment. Although Mr. Davis will always be Cynthia's biological father, he has not shown himself to be a reliable parent and has chosen to not be a part of her life. I love Cynthia very much, and because I am her sole caretaker, I believe she should bear my family name."

After hearing your reasons and any objections, the judge will probably decide on your petition right then and there. However, especially if a child's name change is involved and emotions are running high, the judge may take the matter "under submission" or "under advisement." This is legal jargon for "I'll think about it and tell you what I decide later." If so, the court will notify you by mail of its decision. If you don't hear within a week or so, call the clerk and find out what the court has decided or when it plans to decide.

Steps to Take After Your Name Change

When the court grants your name change petition and signs your Decree, your name change is legally complete. You may want to take a few more steps, however, to make your new name widely known.

Obtain a Certified Copy of the Decree

Some agencies or organizations won't ratify your change without a copy of the Decree officially certified by the court clerk. For a small fee, the court will certify copies of the Decree for you. This means the copies will have a seal that is either raised or printed in blue or purple ink, to verify that it is a true copy of the original. You can obtain certified copies in person or by mail—talk to your court clerk for information. It's a good idea to get a few certified copies.

Amend Your Birth Certificate

After a court-approved name change, you may amend your birth certificate to reflect your new name. If you have changed your gender designation, you can get an entirely new birth certificate. See Chapter 5 for more information if you have done a name change only, or Chapter 7 if you have done a name and gender change.

Notify Agencies and Institutions

If no one knows about the name change, it won't do you any good. Turn to Chapter 10 for information on how to notify people, institutions, and government agencies of your new name.

How to Get Your New Name Accepted

The most important part of accomplishing a name change is having public agencies and private businesses accept your new name. If your identification and records still list you under your old name, your name change (or change of name and gender designation) isn't complete. Although it may take a little time to contact government agencies and businesses, don't be intimidated by the task—it's a common procedure. For example, thousands of people who take their spouses' names when they marry do essentially the same thing every day.

The steps in this chapter apply equally to a change of your name only and to a change of name and gender designation. For ease of reference, we will refer only to change of name as we take you through these steps. Also see "Special Considerations If You've Changed Your Gender," below.

There are three practical steps to implementing a name change:

- Use only your new name.
- Tell your friends and family to call you by your new name only. This change may be the hardest. It will probably take a while for those close to you to make the switch.
- Inform the various government agencies and businesses that you deal with of your name change. See the chart below for help with this process.

Documentation

Assuming that you changed your name by going to court, either by filing a name change petition or including a name change in another proceeding, you already have official documentation of the change: either the Decree Changing Name or an order from a divorce or adoption court changing your name. This document shows that the state has recognized your name change.

Armed with your court order, it should be very easy for you to have your new name accepted. Show this to agencies and institutions that require proof of your name change. Note that a few agencies may want to see, and perhaps keep, a certified copy or your Decree or other order.

If you are changing your name on getting married, your marriage license will serve as your "official" documentation of your name change. Although the certificate does not officially change your name, most agencies and businesses will accept it as proof of your change.

We know that there are some of you who probably have insisted on trying the usage method to change your name. Even though the usage method is still technically legal, for the reasons discussed at length in Chapter 1 we no longer recommend it. For that reason, this chapter is limited to a discussion of how to get your new name accepted after a name change by court petition.

Notify Agencies and Institutions: A Chart

In this section we discuss how to get your name changed in business and government records. This is often the most time-consuming and frustrating part of changing your name. The process involves contacting each business or agency, sometimes in person, and telling them to change your name in their records. We hope the advice we offer here will make the process as smooth as possible.

We recommend that you first obtain a Social Security card in your new name. Then, acquire a driver's license or DMV-issued ID card. (See the chart below for detailed instructions on having your name changed on these or other records.) Once you have these two pieces of identification in your new name, it should be no problem having your other records changed.

TIP

You must get a new Social Security card before going to the DMV. In an effort to curb identity theft, the DMV will not issue a license (or a renewal) unless the name precisely matches the name on your Social Security card.

Agencies and businesses have varying requirements before they will issue new identification for you or change your name in their records. The following chart tells you what the most commonly used agencies require as of 2010. These instructions apply whether you changed your name by a court order or through marriage or divorce.

Most agencies and businesses will want to see certified copies of all court orders and other key legal documents. However, if you changed your name on getting married, you do not need to provide a certified copy of your marriage license. A photocopy of your original should work.

Special Considerations If You've Changed Your Gender

If you have changed both your name and your gender designation, you should follow the instructions in this chart for changing your records—but you may encounter more resistance to the gender change than to the name change. You are probably used to dealing with people who have a hard time accepting your gender change, but in this circumstance you have the legal upper hand: your court order. If someone at any of the agencies described here does not want to make the changes that the court order requires, you should first ask to speak to the person's supervisor, and go as high up in the hierarchy as you need to. Explain that you have a legal court order that requires the agency to conform your records to state your new gender. If you can't get any satisfaction, we suggest you contact either a lawyer, the press, or your local political representatives. If you don't want to make a public fuss, a letter from a lawyer should probably do the trick. To find a transgender-friendly lawyer, contact the Transgender Law Center at www. transgenderlawcenter.org.

Agency or Document	Instructions
Social Security	To obtain a Social Security card in your new name, file an Application for a Social Security Card (Form SS-5). These forms are available on the Social Security Administration's website, www.ssa.gov, at your local Social Security office, or by calling 800-772-1213.
	There is no charge.
	If you already have a Social Security number, use this form to change your name (don't request a new Social Security number). Attach a certified copy of your Decree or other court order. You will probably need to show one additional piece of identification. Acceptable forms of identification include: • employer ID card • passport • school ID card, record, or report card • marriage, divorce, or adoption records • health insurance card • military records, or • insurance policy
	If you are applying for a Social Security number for the first time, you'll also need a certified copy of your birth certificate.
	Even though your Social Security card doesn't list your gender, it's important to change your SSA account to reflect your correct gender. The SSA requires a surgeon or doctor's affidavit verifying a surgical change. If you have questions, contact the Transgender Law Center at www.transgenderlawcenter.org.
Driver's License or California ID card	Go to the local Department of Motor Vehicles and fill out a Form DL-44. Check the box on the form entitled California ID Card "Name Change." You will need to provide one of the following forms of evidence of your new name: • a certified copy of a government-issued document containing your name and date of birth, such as an adoption or divorce order, marriage certificate, domestic partner registration, or name change decree • birth certificate showing your new name • military ID, or • other document considered by the DMV to be a Birthdate/Legal Presence document. These are listed on the DMV website at www.dmv.ca.gov.
	You will need to surrender your current license or ID card and pay the required fee. You will also have to be photographed and give a thumbprint.
	If you do not currently have a driver's license or ID card, you'll need to bring along a Birthdate/Legal Presence document as described above. If you weren't born in the United States, you'll also need proof that you're legally in the country, such as a green card or naturalization papers. (Cal. Veh. Code § 12801.5.)
	Information is available at the DMV website, www.dmv.ca.gov. You can also get a copy of the DL-44 by calling 800-777-0133.
	See Chapter 7 for instructions on changing your gender on your driver's license or ID.

Agency or Document	Instructions
Federal Income Tax	Make arrangements at work for your paychecks, withholding, and W-2 forms to be in your new name. If your employer required you to fill out other Internal Revenue forms, such as an I-9 form verifying eligibility to work, it's a good idea to redo those forms in your new name.
	You are not required to separately contact the IRS about your name change. The revisions you make on your tax forms with your employer will provide notice to the IRS. Simply file your next income tax return using your new name and old Social Security number. (You may file in your new name even if your W-2 is still in your old name, but of course you'll also want to have your employer make the change.)
	A married couple can file a joint income tax form using two different names. Just write your new name(s) on the form. There is space on the tax forms for each spouse's last name.
State Income Tax	Send a letter to Taxpayer Services, Franchise Tax Board, P.O. Box 942840, Sacramento, California 94240-0040. Say that you have changed your name and give your old name, new name, and Social Security number. Use your new name and old Social Security number when filing any later tax returns or forms.
Voting	Register under your new name by completing an Affidavit of Voter Registration; you can get the form at the Registrar of Voters office in your county, or at the DMV, public libraries, post offices, and city offices. You can also register to vote online at www.sos.ca.gov/nvrc/fedform. If you have been registered to vote before, you will need to state the name, address, and political party listed in your most recent registration. Take or mail the completed form to the county Registrar of Voters. Once you've registered, you can vote and sign petitions using your new name.
Passports	The procedures for dealing with passports after a name change have changed recently. You can no longer simply amend your passport; you must have a new one issued.
	If you've had your passport for a year or less, use for DS-5504, Name Change, Data Correction, and Limited Passport Book Replacement Form. Send the completed form, your current passport, a certified copy of your name change order, and two recent identical passport photos to the address shown on the DS-5504 form.
	If you've had your passport longer than a year and it's still valid, you need to use one of two forms. If you: • have your most recent passport • were issued that passport less than 15 years ago, and • were 16 or older when the passport was issued, then you will use form DS-82, Application for a U.S. Passport by Mail. You'll need to submit your original passport, a certified copy of your name change order, two recent identical passport photos, and the required fee ($67).
	If you don't meet those requirements, you'll use Form DS-11, Application for a U.S. Passport, and you'll have to apply in person at a passport application acceptance facility. You'll submit your original passport, a certified copy of your name change order, another form of identification, two recent identical passport photos, and the required fee ($97).

Agency or Document	Instructions
Passports (continued)	You can get forms online at www.travel.state.gov/passport. Or you can go to your local passport office, usually at the main post office in your city, for a copy of the form. There's no fee for renewing if you've had your passport only a year.
	If you have questions, try the website at www.travel.state.gov/passport, or call 1-877-487-2778. You can also write to the passport agency at one of two California main offices: Los Angeles Passport Agency Federal Building, Suite 1000 11000 Wilshire Boulevard Los Angeles, CA 90024-3615 San Francisco Passport Agency 95 Hawthorne Street, 5th Floor San Francisco, CA 94105-3901
	See Chapter 7 for more information about changing your passport after a gender change.
Bank Accounts	Go to your bank in person and tell them you've changed your name. Provide a certified copy of the Decree or other court order. Most banks will also insist on seeing some piece of identification with your new name and photo, such as a driver's license. You will need to sign a new signature card and probably redo all prior documentation to reflect your name change. For a while, banks will probably cross-list you in their records under both your new and old names. If you expect to receive checks made payable to your old name, advise the bank officer. Remember to order checks with your new name.
Credit Cards	Notify your credit card companies of the change and request new cards. To protect your credit history, make sure that the original date of the account is included along with your new name.
	Women's Names. California law provides that no business may refuse to do business with a woman because she uses her birth or former name, regardless of her marital status. (Cal. Civ. Proc. Code § 1279.6.) Credit card companies are required by law to issue credit cards in a woman's birth or married name—the choice of name is entirely up to her. However, the credit card company may insist that a married woman establish an account separate from her husband's. (Cal. Civ. Code § 1747.81.)
	If you have previously been known by your married name, your credit records may be in your husband's name only and may not reflect your credit history. To ensure that you have a credit history in your own name, write to your credit card company and make sure it reports your new name with the original opening date of the joint account.
Public Assistance (Welfare)	Take a certified copy of the Decree or court order to your local welfare office. The office will change its records so you will receive payments under your new name.
	When you complete your monthly reporting statement, indicate that you have changed your name. You can fill in the information in the section that asks whether you have anything else to report.

Agency or Document	Instructions
Birth Certificates and Attachments	Information on California birth certificates and details about when they can be amended or reissued is covered in Chapter 5 (or Chapter 7, if you changed your gender). If you were born outside of California, check with the vital statistics office in the state or country of your birth. Contact information for vital statistics offices can usually be found online.
	If you changed your name by court petition, you can have an amendment attached to your birth certificate reflecting your new name.
Stocks, Bonds, Mutual Funds, Retirement Accounts	If you actually have possession of the stock or bond certificate, you will probably need to send it, along with a signed letter, to the transfer agent listed on the certificate. But it's best to call first and see what their Retirement Accounts exact rules are. Assuming you send a certificate by mail, make a photocopy in case the original is lost. You will receive a certificate in your new name. If, as is more likely, your stock is held in one or more brokerage accounts (you don't have physical possession of the certificates), call the broker to find out the procedures for changing the account. This will normally involve sending them a copy of your certified court decree.
Autos, Boats, and Planes	**Autos and boats.** Changing your driver's license doesn't automatically change your vehicle registration. To have a vehicle reregistered in your new name, complete a "Statement of Facts" (Form REG-256) and file it with your existing title (pink slip) to have a new Certificate of Title issued. On the pink slip, print or type your new name in the "New Registered Owner" section.
	You can download the REG-256 form at www.dmv.ca.gov.
	To change the title, you must be the full legal owner. Or you must contact the institution that holds the title and request that it initiate the name change. This usually isn't necessary until you're ready to sell the vehicle.
	Planes. To change your name on your plane's registration, you'll need to get a Form AC 8050-2 from the FAA's Flight Standards District Office in your area. You can find the FSDO closest to you in the government pages of the phone book or online at www.faa.gov, where you can also download the form. You'll need to fill out the form with your new name and send it along with a $5 fee and a bill of sale or proof of ownership to: FAA Aircraft Registration, P.O. Box 25504, Oklahoma City, OK 73125-0504.
Deeds to Real Estate	If you own real estate, you should change the deed to reflect your new name. This will avoid confusion if you sell or refinance your property. It also will show you did not change your name with the intent of defrauding anyone. You must list both your former and new names on the deed when you sell your property. (Cal. Civ. Code §1096.)
	Here is how to change your deed: Go to a stationery store or a title company and pick up a blank deed that corresponds to your deed (usually a "grant" deed). Or use a copy from *Deeds for California Real Estate*, by Mary Randolph (Nolo). Draw up a new deed following the basic form of your old deed but transferring the property from your former name to your new name. Use wording such as: "[New Name], who acquired title under the former name of [Former Name], hereby grants to [New Name] the following property:" Then include the full legal description of the property.

Agency or Document	Instructions
Deeds to Real Estate (continued)	Above the main part of the deed, there will be a section on transfer tax. If available, check the box before words such as "This transfer is exempt from the documentary transfer tax." Or type in the words "no valuable consideration."
	Sign the deed in your new name and have it notarized. Complete a Preliminary Change of Ownership Report, available from the county recorder or county assessor. Where the form requires transfer information, indicate that the transaction is only a correction of the name on the deed.
	Finally, record your deed with the county recorder's office and pay the small fee. In some courts, you will have to pay an additional fee for file-stamped copies.
Mortgages	Notify the mortgage company of your new name. There is no change in your liability for the mortgage.
Wills, Estate Planning, and Inheritances	**Your Will.** If you have made a will or other estate planning documents, such as a living trust, it is best to avoid confusion by replacing them with new documents reflecting your new name. It's probably best to revise your will anyway, but should you fail to do this, your relatives will not lose their inheritances just because you change your name.
	Someone Else's Will. Don't worry—you won't lose your inheritance by changing your name, even if you are listed in someone's will in your old name. As long as you are the person listed in the will, it makes no difference that your name is different. For example, a woman who changes her name by marriage does not lose any inheritance listed in her birth name. To avoid any confusion, when someone dies who might have left you an inheritance, notify the executor or administrator of the estate of your old and new names.
Insurance	Let your insurance carrier know of your name change. Have policies reissued in your new name. The carrier may request a copy of your court order.
	Automobile insurance. Notify your agent of the name change. Auto insurance rates are not affected by name changes.
	Health insurance. Notify the insurance carrier of the change. If you have coverage through your spouse's employer, your spouse may have to sign a form requesting that a card be issued in your new name under the same coverage.
	Life insurance. Notify the company of the name change if you hold a policy or are the beneficiary of a policy. Should you neglect to notify a company of the name change, it won't alter your right to receive insurance proceeds.
Creditors and Debtors	Obviously, changing your name does not make your debts disappear. Notify your creditors about the change, including holders of promissory notes, medical and legal professionals, landlords, and anyone who has obtained a court judgment against you. You'll need to contact anyone who owes you money, such as renters or debtors against whom you have obtained a court judgment. Notify them of your new name and ask that payments be made in your new name. Changing your name does not affect their debt to you.

Agency or Document	Instructions
Post Office	List both your old and new name on your mailbox, so the carrier will know to deliver mail addressed to you in either name. Eventually, you should receive all mail in your new name and you can remove your old name from the mailbox.
Telephone and Utilities	Contact the telephone company and advise it of the name change. If you want to be listed in the directory under both old and new names, there will be a small monthly charge. Or, more likely, you could arrange to be listed only in your new name.
	Contact your local utility companies and advise them of the name change. If you change both your first and last names, you may have problems with local utilities, especially if they require a deposit for new customers. Let them know you've changed your name but are the same person and can provide them with documentation to that effect. You may then need to send a copy of the Decree or other court order.
School Records	Have your schools change your name on their records in case an employer sends for copies of your grades. (Sunday schools are optional.) You can also petition the school to have your diploma reissued in your new name.
Veterans Administration	Contact the local VA office and let it know you have changed your name. Some offices will accept a letter signed in your new name. Or you can download and fill in Form 21-4138, a blank form put out by the VA and available at www.vba.va.gov/pubs/forms/VBA-21-4138-ARE.pdf. Including a certified copy of the Decree or other court order may be helpful.
Employer's Records	Let your employer know you want to be called only by your new name. Have your name changed in your employment records, including payroll and tax records. If you work as an independent contractor, give your customers your new name.
Legal and Other Important Documents	All important papers should be revised to reflect your new name. This includes legal documents such as durable or regular powers of attorney, living wills, trusts, and contracts.
Other Records	Look through your correspondence, address book, the contents of your wallet, and your important papers to discover if there are other people, businesses, or agencies you must contact. Write a short letter stating that you have legally changed your name and want only your new name to be used from now on. No documentation is needed.

Finding Additional Help

Most name changes are so simple that the average Joe can transform into the average Darren all by himself. However, if your situation turns out to be one of the very rare legally complicated name changes, you may want to do some more research or, in some situations, hire a lawyer.

Even if your name change appears to be routine and uncomplicated, you might want someone else to type up the forms for you. (But don't forget neat hand printing is also an option in most courts.) This is normally easy to accomplish by hiring a nonlawyer legal document preparer. (See "Legal Document Assistants," below.)

Finally, you may want to read up on your right to change your name, or otherwise research the subject of names and name changes. This chapter will be your first step in each of these directions.

When You Might Need a Lawyer

Most name changes are straightforward: An adult asks the court to make the change, the court recognizes the adult's right to go by the name of his or her choosing and grants the name change (usually without the need for a court appearance). The two most common situations in which a petition is more complicated are where someone objects to your name change and where you are petitioning on behalf of a child.

TIP

Most name changes do not require the help of a lawyer. If you are petitioning for a new name on behalf of yourself and can't see someone objecting, you really shouldn't need to hire an attorney.

It is rare to have objections to an adult's name change. As we've seen in this book, though, it can happen. For example, a creditor may think you're trying to avoid payment, or someone who already bears your new name may fear you're planning to use the name for fraudulent purposes. In these situations, you might want an attorney to assist you at the hearing. However, if you have a good handle on your reasons for changing your name and if your opponent's arguments seem easy to refute, you should be able to handle the hearing on your own. And you can save a few dollars by completing the forms yourself.

Changing a child's name is often more complicated than changing an adult's. Usually, no one has an interest in an adult's name besides the adult. On the other hand, many people may have an interest in a child's name and the right to have that opinion heard: the parents, a legal guardian, other relatives, and the child. The court could have an opinion, too. And because more people are typically involved, the chances of someone's objecting are greater. Common situations in which someone disputes a child's proposed name change include:

- You are a recently divorced mother with joint custody of your two daughters. Your daughters are with you five nights per week. You have returned to your birth name and want your little girls to share your last name. Your ex believes that it's premature to change the children's names.

- You share 50/50 custody of your son with your ex-husband. You have been divorced five years and you're both very active in your child's life. You were remarried a year ago and took your new husband's name. You're pregnant again and plan to give your new child your new husband's name. You want your son to share the last name of the rest of your family. However, your former husband believes just as strongly that his son should retain his name, and your son is conflicted about the proposed change.

- You became legal guardian of your close friends' daughter when your friends were tragically killed two years ago. Your new daughter sees a lot of her biological grandparents, but she is now firmly rooted in your nuclear family. You think it would be best for her to share her new family's name, but her grandparents aren't so sure.

In situations like these, a good first step might be mediation. Many cities have community mediation services where volunteer mediators are trained to help resolve conflict before it escalates, for a very modest fee. Try searching on the Internet or in your local phone book to see whether there is a community mediation service in your local area. You can also have a private mediator help you and the objecting family member talk out the disagreement. If you aren't able to resolve everyone's concerns this way, and it looks like the person might go to court to oppose the name change, it may make sense to hire an attorney. These cases will require you to convince the court that a change is in the child's best interests. (See Chapters 4 and 6 for more on children's name changes.) An attorney will be able to fashion arguments, research similar cases, and deal with the other side's attorney. Of course, these are things you could do yourself, but you may conclude that it's worth the cost to hire an expert.

Name change petitions for children can occasionally be problematic even when there are no objections. For instance, you may not know where the child's other parent is, or you may have a strong reason for not wanting to inform the other parent, who has threatened you or the children. In these cases, you might want an attorney to handle only part of the case; for example, the attorney could prepare your application to the court to waive the notice requirement. If you trust yourself to put your arguments down on paper in a clear manner, however, you can handle the other paperwork on your own.

Hiring an Attorney

Finding a knowledgeable lawyer you trust and who charges reasonable prices is not always an easy task. It is natural to feel a little intimidated, but try to remember that a lawyer is simply a service provider you hire to do specific tasks for you. The lawyer will not take over your fundamental decision making. Here are some suggestions for finding and hiring lawyers. You may need to look around for a bit before you find someone you feel comfortable hiring.

Know What You Want Your Lawyer to Do

Before you contact a lawyer, you must decide what you want the lawyer to do. Do you want to hand the entire case over to the lawyer? Or do you want the lawyer to do only a part of the case, such as representing you at the court hearing or making a particular application to the court? Your answer to these questions will depend on how complicated the case is.

In the previous section, we discussed a number of different times in which you might want a lawyer to help you with your name change petition. In each of these, though, you might need the lawyer to do different things:

- If you are changing your own name and believe someone may object, you might be able to do your own paperwork but arrange for a lawyer to help you at the hearing.

- If you are petitioning on behalf of a child and expect objections, you might want an attorney to handle your entire case.
- If you are petitioning on behalf of a child and can't find or don't want to notify the other parent, you might want an attorney to handle your application to waive notice.

Finding a Lawyer

The first thing you should know as you start your attorney search is that few lawyers have a lot of experience with name change petitions. That's because petitioning a court to change a name is such a simple procedure; loads of people do it themselves. The result is that many lawyers in general practice may not know as much about the details of the procedure as is contained in this book. Family lawyers who handle divorce, adoptions, and guardianships are the most likely to be conversant with name change law, especially as it relates to changing the names of women and children.

Talk to Your Friends and Colleagues

One good way to find a lawyer is through a referral from a satisfied and knowledgeable customer. People who have been through a divorce or a custody dispute may be able to supply you with the name of a good family lawyer. If you can only find a referral for an excellent general practice lawyer (or even a lawyer with a different specialty), try calling that lawyer for a recommendation for a family lawyer.

Attorney Referral Services

A lawyer referral service will give you the name of an attorney who practices in your area and handles family law issues. Most county bar associations, which you can find listed in the phone book, operate these services. If you are lucky, you will receive a referral to a competent, experienced person.

Unfortunately, few lawyer referral services do much screening of the attorneys they list, which means those lawyers who participate may not be the most experienced or competent available. Sometimes the lawyers who sign up with referral services are just starting out and need clients. In other instances, they are people who have been practicing for years but want more clients. Be sure to take the time to check out the credentials and experience of the person to whom you're referred.

Online Lawyer Directories

Online lawyer directories are becoming much more common, but many don't provide much information about the attorneys listed. Nolo's Lawyer Directory, at www.nolo.com, contains lengthy profiles of advertisers, which include information about each lawyer's background and education, philosophy of practice— including whether they'll work with self-represented clients—and fee policies.

Other legal websites that include lawyer directories are www.findlaw.com and www.justia.com.

The Martindale-Hubbell Law Directory

The Martindale-Hubbell Law Directory is a big, multi-volume guide that lists most United States lawyers. You can find the complete set in a law library or online at www.martindale.com. You can look up lawyers by name, location, and specialty. Probably the best use of the directory is to find out more about the lawyers whom friends and associates recommend.

Online Document Preparation Services

There are also a number of online services that will prepare your name change documents for you for a fee. These include www.legalzoom.com and www.name changelaw.com.

Dealing With a Lawyer

As we discuss above, you should decide what kind of help you really need before you talk to a lawyer. For example, if you don't make it clear you want limited help, you may find yourself agreeing to turn over your entire name change process at a hefty fee.

Lawyer fees range from $150 to $350 or more per hour. But price is not always related to quality. It depends where you live, but generally, fees of at least $200 to $250 per hour are the norm in urban areas.

In rural areas and smaller cities, $100 to $150 is more like it. It is also common for lawyers to quote fixed fees for simple legal actions such as a name change. For example, a lawyer might agree to handle an adult's name change for $500, $750, or $1,000.

Be sure you settle your fee arrangement —preferably in writing—at the start of your relationship. In addition, you should get a clear, written commitment about the extent of the work the lawyer will handle. For example, if you suspect your petition to change a child's name is likely to be contested, you can ask the lawyer to quote you a firm fixed fee, no matter how many hours the procedure takes.

Legal Document Assistants ("Typing Services")

Until recently, if you didn't hire a lawyer to help with a legal problem, you had two choices: You could handle the problem on your own or not handle it at all. Now, a number of businesses known variously as "legal document assistants," "paralegals," "legal typing services," or "independent paralegals" have emerged to assist people in filling out legal forms. Simple procedures such as name changes, uncontested divorces, and bankruptcies are all routinely handled by these nonlawyer legal document preparation services at a substantially lower cost than lawyers would charge.

These companies are very different from lawyers, because they can't give legal advice or represent you in court. They can, however:

- provide instructions and legal information needed to handle your own name change
- provide the appropriate forms, and
- type your papers so they'll be accepted by a court.

As a general matter, the longer a typing service has been in business, the better. People at the company should be up front with you about not being attorneys and not providing legal advice. A recommendation from someone who has used a particular typing service is the best way to find a reputable one in your area. The services often advertise in classified sections of local newspapers. In California, these services are provided by folks called "legal document preparers" but you may find them listed in the yellow pages under "typing services," "legal services," "paralegals," or "legal document assistants."

Doing Your Own Legal Research

Legal research is how you learn about the law. It is not a skill reserved exclusively for lawyers; you can find the answers to your legal questions yourself if you are armed with a little bit of patience and a good road map. The best legal research method depends on what you need to find out.

Fortunately, the law governing name changes is not particularly difficult to research. You probably won't need to go beyond some California laws (statutes) and, in some instances, court cases interpreting these laws. But first, you'll need a law library or a computer with online access.

Going to the Law Library

Every California county maintains a law library that is required to serve all members of the public—not just lawyers and judges. Although some libraries have more books than others, all have the California statutes, written court opinions, and expert commentary. Some larger public libraries also have extensive collections of law and legal research books. Before making a special trip to the law library, you may first want to check with your main branch public library.

When you get to the library, you'll probably need the help of a good legal research guidebook and a kind reference librarian. Thankfully, law librarians are almost always helpful and courteous to nonlawyers doing their own legal research.

Looking Up Statutes

State statutes are laws passed by the state legislature. This book includes many numbered references to California statutes. California's statutes are organized by topic, such as the Civil Code, Code of Civil Procedure, Family Code, and Health and Safety Code. Most laws having to do with

name changes are in the Code of Civil Procedure.

Every law library and some regular public libraries will have copies of these California codes. You can also find the statutes online. One easy place to find them is through Nolo's website, at www.nolo.com/legal-research.

When you look for statutes (also called the state code) at the library, you'll find them in two versions: books containing only the laws themselves, and books with "annotated" codes. The annotated version can be helpful when you are dealing with more complicated legal issues, because it includes summaries of court opinions (cases) interpreting the law and other resources following the text of each law. But the case law summaries are just that, so read the full text of the court decision yourself rather than just relying on the summary.

Looking Up Cases

"Case law" refers to a court's written opinion resolving one or more issues of a particular lawsuit. Court opinions, also called cases, do one of two things. First, courts interpret statutes, regulations, and ordinances so that we know how they apply in real-life situations. Second, courts make rules that are not found in statutes, regulations, or ordinances. Often these decisions are in areas not clearly covered by a statute. These court-made laws are called the "common law."

California Courts Approve the Usage Method

The right to change your name without going to court is a common law right. It was created by the courts rather than the legislature. This means that none of the state statutes say specifically that you can change your name without going to court. But a number of cases say just this, including *In re Marriage of Banks*, 42 Cal. App. 3d 631 (1974), which states, "A person may change his name at any time without initiating legal proceedings." To learn about your right to change your name without going to court, you'll have to read cases such as *Banks*. If you can find a case with facts similar to your situation, you can get some guidance on how a court might decide your case.

If you wish to do more research on your right to change your name via the usage method, check out the following California court decisions: *Lee v. Ventura County Superior Court*, 9 Cal. App. 4th 510, 513, 11 Cal. Rptr. 2d 763 (1992); *Cabrera v. McMullen*, 204 Cal. App. 3d 1 (1988); *In re Ritchie*, 159 Cal. App. 3d 1070 (1984); *In re Marriage of Banks*, 42 Cal. App. 3d 631 (1974); *Sousa v. Freitas*, 10 Cal. App. 3d 660 (1970); *Application of Trower*, 260 Cal. App. 2d 75 (1968). All basically state that the court procedure for changing one's name does not affect the right of California adults to change their names without going to court.

> **CAUTION**
> Despite this common law right and the holdings in the cases cited below, we still believe that the usage method is no longer a viable way to change your name in California.

California cases are published in four different sets of books: California Reports ("Cal.") covers cases from the California Supreme Court; California Appellate Reports ("Cal. App.") publishes appellate court cases; California Reporter ("Cal. Rptr.") includes both Supreme and appellate court cases; and the Pacific Reporter ("P.") publishes Supreme and pre-1960 appellate court cases, along with cases from the other Western states.

A "case citation" is a shorthand identification of the volume, series of reporter, and page number where the case can be found. Or put another way, a citation is a case's address: It tells you where to find it. Take as an example the *Banks* case, listed above. Its citation is 42 Cal. App. 3d 631 (1974); this tells you it is in Volume 42 of California Appellate Reports (third series) on page 631. Each citation has the same format: volume, reporter (including series), and page. One case can have a few different citations, because it may be listed in a few different reporters. The citation will list the reporter by the abbreviation listed in parentheses after each reporter's name, above.

You can also find many California cases online. One of the best websites for researching case law is FindLaw (www .findlaw.com). At the time of this printing, you can find the cases listed above free of charge, though you will have to register with the website.

 RESOURCE

Legal Research: How to Find & Understand the Law, by Stephen Elias and the Editors of Nolo (Nolo), is a hands-on guide to the law library, including online resources. It addresses research methods in detail and should answer most questions that arise in the course of your research. It also contains a good discussion of how to read and analyze statutes.

Online Legal Research

Another way to approach legal research is to use a computer. If you want the text of a California statute, information about a recent court decision, or a copy of a legal form, you'll probably be able to find it on the Internet.

You may want to start by visiting Nolo's site, at www.nolo.com. We offer extensive material on a wide variety of legal subjects, including more information about doing your own legal research, on paper and online. We also have links to California statutes and to county courthouses across California. You can use this feature to find a copy of your local Superior Court's local rules. As we mention in Chapter 6, local rules govern particulars like which branch court you should file with (if your court has branches) and the exact form your papers should be in for the court to accept them.

Here are some other websites to help you find legal resources:

- **Court Rules.** California Judicial Council (www.courtinfo.ca.gov/rules).
- **Statutes.** Legislative Council of California (www.leginfo.ca.gov/calaw .html).
- **Cases.** FindLaw (www.findlaw.com); WestLaw (www.westlaw.com).
- **Legal Forms.** California Judicial Council (www.courtinfo.ca.gov/ forms).

How to Use the CD-ROM

The CD-ROM included with this book can be used with Windows computers. It installs files that use software programs that need to be on your computer already. It is not a stand-alone software program.

In accordance with U.S. copyright laws, the CD-ROM and its files are for your personal use only.

Please read this appendix and the Readme.htm file included on the CD-ROM for instructions on using it. For a list of files and their file names, see the end of this appendix.

Note to Macintosh users: This CD-ROM and its files should also work on Macintosh computers. Please note, however, that Nolo cannot provide technical support for non-Windows users.

Note to eBook users: You can access the CD-ROM files mentioned here from the bookmarked section of the eBook, located on the left-hand side.

Installing the Files Onto Your Computer

To work with the files on the CD-ROM, you first need to install them onto your hard disk. Here's how:

Windows XP, Vista, and 7

Follow the CD-ROM's instructions that appear on the screen.

If nothing happens when you insert the CD-ROM, then:

How to View the README File

To view the "Readme.htm" file, insert the CD-ROM into your computer's CD-ROM drive and follow these instructions:

Windows XP, Vista, and 7
1. On your PC's desktop, double-click the **My Computer** icon.
2. Double-click the icon for the CD-ROM drive into which the CD-ROM was inserted.
3. Double-click the file "Readme.htm."

Macintosh
1. On your Mac desktop, double-click the icon for the CD-ROM that you inserted.
2. Double-click the file Readme.htm.

3. Double-click the **My Computer** icon.
4. Double-click the icon for the CD-ROM drive into which the CD-ROM was inserted.
5. Double-click the file "Setup.exe."

Macintosh

If the **Name Change CD** window is not open, double-click the **Name Change CD** icon. Then:
1. Select the **Name Change Forms** folder icon.
2. Drag and drop the folder icon onto your computer.

Where Are the Files Installed?

Windows

By default, all the files are installed to the **Name Change Forms** folder in the **Program Files** folder of your computer. A folder called **Name Change Forms** is added to the **Programs** folder of the **Start** menu.

Macintosh

All the files are located in the **Name Change Forms** folder.

Using Government Forms

The CD-ROM includes government forms in PDF format. These form files were created by the government, not by Nolo.

To use them, you need Adobe *Reader* installed on your computer. If you don't already have this software, you can download it for free at www.adobe.com.

Some of these forms have fill-in text fields. To use them:

1. Open a file.
2. Fill in the text fields using either your mouse or the TAB key to navigate from field to field.
3. Print out the form.

Opening a Form

PDF files, like the word processing files, can be opened any of the three following ways:

- Windows users can open a file by selecting its "shortcut."
  1. Click the Windows **Start** button.
  2. Open the **Programs** folder.
  3. Open the **Name Change Forms** subfolder.
  4. Click the shortcut to the form you want to work with.
- Both Windows and Macintosh users can open a file directly by double-clicking it.
  1. Use **My Computer** or **Windows Explorer** (Windows XP, Vista, or 7) or the Finder (Macintosh) to go to the folder you created and copied the CD-ROM's files to.
  2. Double-click the specific file you want to open.
- Both Windows and Macintosh users can open a PDF file from within Adobe *Reader*.
  1. Open Adobe *Reader*.
  2. Go to the **File** menu and choose the **Open** command. This opens a dialog box.
  3. Tell the program the location and name of the file (you will need to navigate through the directory tree to get to the folder on your hard disk where the CD's files have been installed).

For further assistance, check Adobe *Reader*'s help. Nolo's technical support department is unable to help with the use of Adobe *Reader*.

Filling in a Form

Newer government forms enable you to fill in your form on your computer using Adobe *Reader* 5.1 or higher. If this feature is available, when you open the form you will see a message box about document rights. If you are using an earlier version of Adobe *Reader*, you will be prompted to download a newer version.

Use your mouse or the TAB key to navigate from field to field within these forms.

To complete forms without fill-in fields, print them and fill them in either by hand or with a typewriter.

Saving a Filled-In Form

If document rights are enabled, after completing your form onscreen, you can save it using Adobe *Reader* 5.1 or higher. If document rights are not enabled, although you cannot save the form, you can print it out.

Using the Spreadsheets

This section concerns the spreadsheet file, which is in Microsoft's Excel format and has the extension ".xls." The Missing Parent Search Log spreadsheet, discussed in Chapter 8, is on the file SearchLog.xls. It can be opened and edited with Microsoft's Excel and other spreadsheet programs that read XLS files.

The following are general instructions. Because each spreadsheet program uses different commands to open, format, save, and print documents, read your spreadsheet program's help files for specific instructions. Nolo's technical support department is unable to assist with your spreadsheet software.

To complete a spreadsheet,
1. open the file in a spreadsheet program that is compatible with XLS files;
2. fill in the needed fields;
3. print it out;
4. rename and save your revised file.

Opening a File

There are three ways to open the spreadsheet.
- Windows users can open a file by selecting its shortcut.
  1. Click the Windows **Start** button;
  2. open the **Programs** folder;
  3. open the **Name Change Forms** subfolder; and
  4. click the shortcut.
- Both Windows and Macintosh users can open a file by double-clicking it. Use My Computer or Windows Explorer (Windows Vista, XP, 7) or the Finder (Macintosh) to go to the **Name**

Change Forms folder you installed on your computer. Then, double-click the file you want to open.

- Windows and Macintosh users can open a file from within your spreadsheet program. To do this,
  1. start your spreadsheet program;
  2. go to the **File** menu and choose the **Open** command. This opens a dialog box where
  3. you will select the location and name of the file. (You will navigate to the **Name Change Forms** folder that you installed on your computer.)

Entering Information Into the Spreadsheet

While you are filling in information, you can consult the instructions and sample spreadsheets in the book for help.

Printing Out the Spreadsheet

Use your spreadsheet program's **Print** command to print out your document.

Saving Your Spreadsheet

After filling in the form, use **Save As** and rename the file. You will be unable to use the **Save** command because the files are "read-only." If you were to save the file without renaming it, it would overwrite the original spreadsheet, and you would need to recopy the original file from the CD-ROM to create a new document.

Forms on the CD-ROM

The following forms are included in Portable Document Format (PDF).

File Name	Form Title
fl395.pdf	Ex Parte Application for Restoration of Former Name After Entry of Judgment and Order
nc100.pdf	Petition for Change of Name
nc110.pdf	Name and Information About the Person Whose Name Is to Be Changed: Attachment to Petition (form NC-100 or form NC-200)
nc120.pdf	Order to Show Cause for Change of Name
nc130.pdf	Decree Changing Name
cm010.pdf	Civil Case Cover Sheet
nc110g.pdf	Declaration of Guardian: Supplemental Attachment to Petition for Change of Name (Form NC-100)
nc130g.pdf	Decree Changing Name of Minor by Guardian
nc200.pdf	Petition for Change of Name and Gender
nc210.pdf	Declaration of Physician Documenting Change of Gender Through Surgical Treatment Under Health and Safety Codes Sections 103425 and 103430
nc220.pdf	Order to Show Cause for Change of Name and Gender
nc230.pdf	Decree Changing Name and Gender
nc300.pdf	Petition for Change of Gender and Issuance of New Birth Certificate
nc320.pdf	Notice of Hearing on Petition for Change of Gender and Issuance of New Birth Certificate
nc330.pdf	Order for Change of Gender and Issuance of New Birth Certificate
fw001info.pdf	Information Sheet on Waiver of Court Fees and Costs
fw001.pdf	Request to Waive Court Fees
mc025.pdf	Attachment to Judicial Council Form
fw003.pdf	Order on Court Fee Waiver
fw006.pdf	Request for Hearing About Court Fee Waiver
fw008.pdf	Order on Court Fee Waiver After Hearing
nc121.pdf	Proof of Service of Order to Show Cause by Personal Delivery/Mailing (Outside California Only)
mc030.pdf	Declaration
mc020.pdf	Additional Page: Attach to Judicial Council Form or Other Court Paper
pleading.pdf	Pleading paper

The following form is an Excel spreadsheet.

File Name	Form Title
SearchLog.xls	Missing Parent Search Log

Sample Blank Forms

Chapter	Form Number	Form Title
4	FL-395	Ex Parte Application for Restoration of Former Name After Entry of Judgment and Order
6	NC-100	Petition for Change of Name
6	NC-110	Attachment to Petition for Change of Name
6	NC-120	Order to Show Cause for Change of Name
6	NC-130	Decree Changing Name
6	CM-010	Civil Case Cover Sheet
6	NC-110G	Supplemental Attachment to Petition for Change of Name (Declaration of Guardian)
6	NC-130G	Decree Changing Name of Minor (by Guardian)
7	NC-200	Petition for Change of Name and Gender
7	NC-210/310	Declaration of Physician Documenting Change of Gender Through Surgical Treatment Under Health and Safety Code Sections 103425 and 103430
7	NC-220	Order to Show Cause for Change of Name and Gender
7	NC-230	Decree Changing Name and Gender
7	DL-329	Medical Certification and Authorization (Gender Change)
7	NC-300	Petition for Change of Gender and Issuance of New Birth Certificate
7	NC-320	Notice of Hearing on Petition for Change of Gender and Issuance of New Birth Certificate
7	NC-330	Order for Change of Gender and Issuance of New Birth Certificate
8	FW-001-INFO	Information Sheet on Waiver of Superior Court Fees and Costs
8	FW-001	Request to Waive Court Fees
8	MC-025	Attachment
8	FW-003	Order on Court Fee Waiver
8	FW-006	Request for Hearing About Court Fee Waiver
8	FW-008	Order on Court Fee Waiver After Hearing
8	NC-121	Proof of Service of Order to Show Cause
8		Missing Parent Search Log
8	MC-030	Declaration

This appendix shows all of the forms you will need to complete your name change. All of the forms used in Chapters 4, 6, 7, and 8 are designed by the California Judicial Council, and all were current when we prepared this book (September 2007). However, the Council changes its forms from time to time. To learn whether a form has been updated, turn to the form in the appendix and look for its number and revision date, which you'll find in the lower left-hand corner. Go to the Judicial Council's website (www.courtinfo.ca.gov/forms) and view the forms by number. Look for your form, select it, and compare its date with the date on the form in this book. Also, check the site's listing of "Recent Form Changes." If the form on the site has a more recent date than the one in this book, download the form and use it. Do not attempt to use an old form.

FL-395

ATTORNEY OR PARTY WITHOUT ATTORNEY *(Name and Address):*	TELEPHONE NO.:	*FOR COURT USE ONLY*

ATTORNEY FOR *(Name):*

SUPERIOR COURT OF CALIFORNIA, COUNTY OF
STREET ADDRESS:
MAILING ADDRESS:
CITY AND ZIP CODE:
BRANCH NAME:

MARRIAGE OF
PETITIONER:

RESPONDENT:

EX PARTE APPLICATION FOR RESTORATION OF FORMER NAME AFTER ENTRY OF JUDGMENT AND ORDER	CASE NUMBER:

APPLICATION

1. A judgment of dissolution or nullity was entered on *(date):*

2. Applicant now requests that his or her former name be restored. The applicant's former name is *(specify):*

Date:

_____   ▶   _____
(TYPE OR PRINT NAME)   (SIGNATURE OF APPLICANT)
                                                                                     (USE CURRENT NAME)

ORDER

3. IT IS ORDERED that applicant's former name is restored to *(specify):*

Date:

_____
JUDICIAL OFFICER

[SEAL]	**CLERK'S CERTIFICATE**

I certify that the foregoing is a true and correct copy of the original on file in my office.

Date: _____   Clerk, by _____ , Deputy

Page 1 of 1

Form Adopted for Mandatory Use
Judicial Council of California
FL-395 [Rev. January 1, 2003]

EX PARTE APPLICATION FOR RESTORATION OF FORMER NAME AFTER ENTRY OF JUDGMENT AND ORDER (Family Law)

Family Code, § 2080
www.courtinfo.ca.gov

NC-100

ATTORNEY OR PARTY WITHOUT ATTORNEY *(Name, State Bar number, and address):*	*FOR COURT USE ONLY*
TELEPHONE NO.:　　　　FAX NO. *(Optional):*	
E-MAIL ADDRESS *(Optional):*	
ATTORNEY FOR *(Name):*	

SUPERIOR COURT OF CALIFORNIA, COUNTY OF

STREET ADDRESS:

MAILING ADDRESS:

CITY AND ZIP CODE:

BRANCH NAME:

PETITION OF *(Name of each petitioner):*

PETITION FOR CHANGE OF NAME	CASE NUMBER:

Before you complete this petition, you should read the *Instructions for Filing a Petition for Change of Name* on the next page. You must answer all questions and check all boxes on this petition that apply to you. You must file this petition in the superior court of the county where the person whose name is to be changed resides.

1. Petitioner *(name):*　　　　　　　　　　　　　　　　　　　resides in this county.

2. Petitioner requests that the court decree the following name changes *(list every name that you are seeking to change):*

   <u>Present name</u>　　　　　　　　　　　　　　　　<u>Proposed name</u>

   a. _____ changed to _____

   b. _____ changed to _____

   c. _____ changed to _____

   d. _____ changed to _____

   ☐ Continued *(if you are seeking to change additional names, you must prepare a list and attach it to this petition as Attachment 2).*

3. Petitioner requests that the court issue an order directing all interested persons to appear and show cause why this petition for change of name of the persons identified in item 2 should not be granted.

4. The number of persons under 18 years of age whose names are to be changed is *(specify):* _____

5. If this petition requests the change of name of any person or persons under 18 years, this request is being made by

   a. ☐ both parents.

   b. ☐ mother only.

   c. ☐ father only.

   d. ☐ near relative *(name and relationship):*

   e. ☐ guardian *(name):*

   f. ☐ other *(specify):*

6. For each person whose name is to be changed, petitioner provides the following information *(you must attach a completed copy of the attachment Name and Information About the Person Whose Name Is to Be Changed (form NC-110) for each person identified in item 2):*

   a. The number of attachments included in this petition is *(specify number):* _____

   b–f. *(Attachment page or pages)*

(Instructions on next page)　　　　　　　　　　　　　　　　　　　　　　**Page 1 of 2**

Form Adopted for Mandatory Use
Judicial Council of California
NC-100 [Rev. January 1, 2010]

PETITION FOR CHANGE OF NAME
(Change of Name)

Code of Civil Procedure, § 1275 et seq.
www.courtinfo.ca.gov

INSTRUCTIONS FOR FILING A PETITION
FOR CHANGE OF NAME

1. **Where to File**

   The petition for change of name must be filed in the superior court of the county where the person whose name is to be changed presently lives.

2. **Whose Name May Be Changed**

   The petition may be used to change one's own name and, under certain circumstances, the names of others (e.g., children under 18 years of age).

3. **Confidentiality of Certain Names**

   In cases in which the petitioner is a participant in the Secretary of State's address confidentiality program (Safe at Home), petitioner's current and proposed names may be kept confidential. (Code Civ. Proc., § 1277(b).) See *Information Sheet for Name Change Proceedings Under Address Confidentiality Program (Safe at Home)* (form NC-400-INFO) for additional instructions when such confidentiality is desired.

4. **What Forms Are Required**

   Prepare an original and two copies of each of the following documents:

   a. *Petition for Change of Name* (form NC-100)

   b. *Name and Information About the Person Whose Name Is to Be Changed (Attachment to Petition)* (form NC-110) (attach as many copies as necessary)

   c. *Order to Show Cause for Change of Name* (form NC-120)

   d. *Decree Changing Name* (form NC-130 or, for guardians, form NC-130G)

   In addition, a guardian must prepare and attach a *Declaration of Guardian (Supplemental Attachment to Petition)* (form NC-110G) for each child whose name is to be changed.

5. **Filing and Filing Fee**

   Prepare an original *Civil Case Cover Sheet* (form CM-010). File the original petition and *Civil Case Cover Sheet* with the clerk of the court and obtain two filed-endorsed copies of the petition. A filing fee will be charged unless you qualify for a fee waiver. (If you want to apply for a fee waiver, see *Application for Waiver of Court Fees and Costs* (form FW-001); *Information Sheet on Waiver of Court Fees and Costs* (form FW-001-INFO); and *Order on Application for Waiver of Court Fees and Costs* (form FW-003.)

6. **Requesting a Court Hearing Date and Obtaining the Order to Show Cause**

   You should request a date for the hearing on the *Order to Show Cause* at least six weeks in the future. Take the completed form to the clerk's office. The clerk will provide the hearing date and location, obtain the judicial officer's signature, file the original, and give you a copy.

7. **Publishing the Order to Show Cause**

   In most cases, a copy of the *Order to Show Cause* must be published in a local newspaper of general circulation once a week for **at least four consecutive weeks** before the date of the hearing. The petitioner selects the newspaper from among those newspapers legally qualified to publish orders and notices. The newspaper used must file a Proof of Publication with the superior court before the hearing. If no newspaper of general circulation is published in the county, the court may order the *Order to Show Cause* to be posted by the clerk. But petitioners do not have to publish the order if they are participants in (1) the State Witness Program or (2) in the address confidentiality program and the petition alleges that they are (a) petitioning to avoid domestic violence, or (b) petitioning to avoid stalking, or (c) the petitioner is, or is filing on behalf of, a victim of sexual assault.

8. **Name Change for Children**

   a. If a petitioning parent is requesting the name change for a child under 18 years of age, and one of the parents, if living, does not join in consenting to the name change, the petitioning parent must have a copy of the *Order to Show Cause* or notice of the time and place of the hearing served on the nonconsenting parent. Service must be made **at least 30 days prior to the hearing** under Code of Civil Procedure section 413.10, 414.10, 415.10, or 415.40.

   b. If the nonconsenting parent resides in California, the order or notice must be personally served on the nonconsenting parent. The petitioning parent cannot personally serve this document.

   c. If the nonconsenting parent resides outside California, he or she may be served by sending a copy of the order or notice by first-class mail, postage prepaid, return receipt requested.

   d. If a petition to change the name of a child has been filed by a guardian, the guardian must (1) provide notice of the hearing to any living parent of the child by personal service at least 30 days before the hearing, or (2) if either or both parents are deceased or cannot be located, serve notice of the hearing on the child's grandparents, if living, not less than 30 days before the hearing under Code of Civil Procedure section 413.10, 414.10, 415.10, or 415.40.

   If you have served a parent or grandparents, file a copy of the completed *Proof of Service of Order to Show Cause* (form NC-121) with the court before the hearing.

9. **Court Hearing**

   If no written objection is filed at least two court days before the hearing, the court may grant the petition without a hearing. Check with the court to find out if a hearing will be held. If there is a hearing, bring copies of all documents to the hearing. If the judge grants the petition, the judge will sign the original decree.

10. If you want to amend a birth certificate to show the name change, you should contact the following office:

    California Department of Health Services, Office of Vital Records
    MS 5103, P.O. Box 997410, Sacramento, CA 95899-7410
    Phone: (916) 445-2684, Web site: www.dhs.ca.gov

Local courts may supplement these instructions. Check with the court to determine whether supplemental information is available. For instance, the court may provide you with additional written information identifying the department that handles name change petitions, the times when petitions are heard, and the newspapers that may be used to publish the *Order to Show Cause.*

PETITION FOR CHANGE OF NAME
(Change of Name)

NC-110

PETITION OF (Name of petitioner or petitioners):	CASE NUMBER:
FOR CHANGE OF NAME	

NAME AND INFORMATION ABOUT THE PERSON
WHOSE NAME IS TO BE CHANGED
Attachment to *Petition* (form NC-100 or form NC-200)

Attachment _____ of _____

*(You must use a **separate** attachment for **each person** whose name is to be changed. If petitioner is a guardian of a minor, a supplemental attachment, Declaration of Guardian (form NC-110G), must also be completed and attached for each minor whose name is to be changed.)*

6. *(Continued)* Petitioner applies for a decree to change the name of the following person:

   b. ☐ Self ☐ Other

      (1) Present name *(specify)*:

      (2) Proposed name *(specify)*:

      (3) Born on *(date of birth)*:

         and presently ☐ under 18 years of age ☐ over 18 years of age

      (4) Born at *(place of birth)*:

      (5) Sex *(as stated on original birth certificate)*: ☐ Male ☐ Female

      (6) Current residence address *(street, city, county, and zip code)*:

   c. Reason for name change *(explain)*:

   d. Relationship of the petitioner to the person whose name will be changed:

      (1) ☐ self   (4) ☐ near relative *(indicate relationship)*:

      (2) ☐ parent   (5) ☐ other *(specify)*:

      (3) ☐ guardian

   e. If the person whose name will be changed is under 18 years of age, provide the names and addresses, if known, of the following persons:

      (1) Father *(name)*:   *(address)*:

      (2) Mother *(name)*:   *(address)*:

      (3) *(Only if neither parent is living)* Near relatives *(names, relationships, and addresses)*:

   f. If the person whose name will be changed is 18 years of age or older, that person must sign the following declaration:

DECLARATION

I declare under penalty of perjury under the laws of the State of California that ☐ I am not ☐ I am under the jurisdiction of the California Department of Corrections (in state prison or on parole) **and** ☐ I am not ☐ I am required to register as a sex offender under Penal Code section 290.

Date:

▶

(TYPE OR PRINT NAME OF PERSON WHOSE NAME IS TO BE CHANGED)	(SIGNATURE OF PERSON WHOSE NAME IS TO BE CHANGED)

(If petitioner is represented by an attorney, the attorney's signature follows):

Date:

▶

(TYPE OR PRINT NAME)	(SIGNATURE OF ATTORNEY)

(Each petitioner must sign this petition in the space provided below or, if additional pages are attached, at the end of the last attachment.) I declare under penalty of perjury under the laws of the State of California that the information in the foregoing petition is true and correct.

Date:

▶

(TYPE OR PRINT NAME)	(SIGNATURE OF PETITIONER)

Date:

▶

(TYPE OR PRINT NAME)	(SIGNATURE OF PETITIONER)

☐ ADD ADDITIONAL SIGNATURE LINES FOR ADDITIONAL PETITIONERS   ☐ SIGNATURE OF PETITIONERS FOLLOWS LAST ATTACHMENT

Form Adopted for Mandatory Use
Judicial Council of California
NC-110 [Rev. January 1, 2003]

ATTACHMENT TO
PETITION FOR CHANGE OF NAME

Code of Civil Procedure, § 1275 et seq.

NC-120

PETITIONER OR ATTORNEY *(Name, State Bar number, and address):*

TELEPHONE NO.:   FAX NO. *(Optional):*

E-MAIL ADDRESS *(Optional):*

ATTORNEY FOR *(Name):*

SUPERIOR COURT OF CALIFORNIA, COUNTY OF

STREET ADDRESS:

MAILING ADDRESS:

CITY AND ZIP CODE:

BRANCH NAME:

PETITION OF *(Name of each petitioner):*

FOR CHANGE OF NAME

ORDER TO SHOW CAUSE FOR CHANGE OF NAME	CASE NUMBER:

TO ALL INTERESTED PERSONS:

1. Petitioner *(name):*   filed a petition with this court

for a decree changing names as follows:

	Present name		Proposed name
a.	_____	to	_____
b.	_____	to	_____
c.	_____	to	_____
d.	_____	to	_____
e.	_____	to	_____

☐ Continued on Attachment 1.

2. THE COURT ORDERS that all persons interested in this matter appear before this court at the hearing indicated below to show cause, if any, why the petition for change of name should not be granted. Any person objecting to the name changes described above must file a written objection that includes the reasons for the objection at least two court days before the matter is scheduled to be heard and must appear at the hearing to show cause why the petition should not be granted. If no written objection is timely filed, the court may grant the petition without a hearing.

NOTICE OF HEARING

a. Date: _____ Time: _____ ☐ Dept.: _____ ☐ Room: _____

b. The address of the court is ☐ same as noted above ☐ other *(specify):*

3. a. ☐ A copy of this *Order to Show Cause* shall be published at least once each week for four successive weeks prior to the date set for hearing on the petition in the following newspaper of general circulation, printed in this county *(specify newspaper):*

b. ☐ Other *(specify):*

Date: _____

_____

JUDGE OF THE SUPERIOR COURT

> **NOTE:** When a *Petition for Change of Name* has been filed for a child and the other parent, if living, does not join in consenting to the name change, the petitioner must have a notice of the time and place of the hearing or a copy of the *Order to Show Cause* served on the other parent not less than 30 days prior to the hearing under Code of Civil Procedure section 413.10, 414.10, 415.10, or 415.40. If a petition to change the name of a child has been filed by a guardian, the guardian must (1) provide notice of the hearing to any living parent of the child by personal service at least 30 days before the hearing, or (2) if either or both parents are deceased or cannot be located, serve notice of the hearing on the child's grandparents, if living, not less than 30 days before the hearing under Code of Civil Procedure section 413.10, 414.10, 415.10, or 415.40. *(This Note is included for the information of the petitioner and shall not be included in the Order to Show Cause published in the newspaper.)*

Form Adopted for Mandatory Use
Judicial Council of California
NC-120 [Rev. July 1, 2007]

**ORDER TO SHOW CAUSE
FOR CHANGE OF NAME
(Change of Name)**

Code of Civil Procedure, § 1277

NC-130

PETITIONER OR ATTORNEY *(Name, State Bar number, and address)*:

TELEPHONE NO.   FAX NO. *(Optional)*:
E-MAIL ADDRESS *(Optional)*:
ATTORNEY FOR *(Name)*:

SUPERIOR COURT OF CALIFORNIA, COUNTY OF
    STREET ADDRESS
    MAILING ADDRESS:
    CITY AND ZIP CODE:
    BRANCH NAME:

PETITION OF *(Name of each petitioner)*:

                    FOR CHANGE OF NAME

DECREE CHANGING NAME	CASE NUMBER:

1. The petition was duly considered:
   a. ☐ at the hearing on *(date)*:   in Courtroom: of the above-entitled court.
   b. ☐ without hearing.

THE COURT FINDS

2. a. All notices required by law have been given.
   b. Each person whose name is to be changed identified in item 3 below
     (1) ☐ is not ☐ is under the jurisdiction of the Department of Corrections, and
     (2) ☐ is not ☐ is required to register as a sex offender under section 290 of the Penal Code.
     These determinations were made ☐ by using CLETS/CJIS ☐ based on information provided to the clerk of the court by a local law enforcement agency.
   c. ☐ No objections to the proposed change of name were made.
   d. ☐ Objections to the proposed change of name were made by *(name)*:

   e. it appears to the satisfaction of the court that all the allegations in the petition are true and sufficient and that the petition should be granted.
   f. ☐ Other findings (if *any*):

THE COURT ORDERS

3. The name of

               Present name   New name

   a. _____ is changed to _____
   b. _____ is changed to _____
   c. _____ is changed to _____
   d. _____ is changed to _____
   e. _____ is changed to _____

   ☐ Additional name changes are listed on Attachment 3.

Date: _____

                            JUDGE OF THE SUPERIOR COURT
              ☐ SIGNATURE OF JUDGE FOLLOWS LAST ATTACHMENT

Form Adopted for Mandatory Use Judicial Council of California NC-130 [Rev. July 1, 2007]	**DECREE CHANGING NAME** (Change of Name)	Code of Civil Procedure, §§ 1278, 1279

CM-010

ATTORNEY OR PARTY WITHOUT ATTORNEY *(Name, State Bar number, and address):*	
TELEPHONE NO.: FAX NO.:	
ATTORNEY FOR *(Name):*	

SUPERIOR COURT OF CALIFORNIA, COUNTY OF
STREET ADDRESS:
MAILING ADDRESS:
CITY AND ZIP CODE:
BRANCH NAME:

CASE NAME:

CIVIL CASE COVER SHEET		Complex Case Designation	CASE NUMBER:
☐ Unlimited ☐ Limited		☐ Counter ☐ Joinder	
(Amount demanded exceeds $25,000)	(Amount demanded is $25,000 or less)	Filed with first appearance by defendant (Cal. Rules of Court, rule 3.402)	JUDGE: DEPT:

Items 1–6 below must be completed (see instructions on page 2).

1. Check **one** box below for the case type that best describes this case:

Auto Tort
☐ Auto (22)
☐ Uninsured motorist (46)

Other PI/PD/WD (Personal Injury/Property Damage/Wrongful Death) Tort
☐ Asbestos (04)
☐ Product liability (24)
☐ Medical malpractice (45)
☐ Other PI/PD/WD (23)

Non-PI/PD/WD (Other) Tort
☐ Business tort/unfair business practice (07)
☐ Civil rights (08)
☐ Defamation (13)
☐ Fraud (16)
☐ Intellectual property (19)
☐ Professional negligence (25)
☐ Other non-PI/PD/WD tort (35)

Employment
☐ Wrongful termination (36)
☐ Other employment (15)

Contract
☐ Breach of contract/warranty (06)
☐ Rule 3.740 collections (09)
☐ Other collections (09)
☐ Insurance coverage (18)
☐ Other contract (37)

Real Property
☐ Eminent domain/Inverse condemnation (14)
☐ Wrongful eviction (33)
☐ Other real property (26)

Unlawful Detainer
☐ Commercial (31)
☐ Residential (32)
☐ Drugs (38)

Judicial Review
☐ Asset forfeiture (05)
☐ Petition re: arbitration award (11)
☐ Writ of mandate (02)
☐ Other judicial review (39)

Provisionally Complex Civil Litigation (Cal. Rules of Court, rules 3.400–3.403)
☐ Antitrust/Trade regulation (03)
☐ Construction defect (10)
☐ Mass tort (40)
☐ Securities litigation (28)
☐ Environmental/Toxic tort (30)
☐ Insurance coverage claims arising from the above listed provisionally complex case types (41)

Enforcement of Judgment
☐ Enforcement of judgment (20)

Miscellaneous Civil Complaint
☐ RICO (27)
☐ Other complaint *(not specified above)* (42)

Miscellaneous Civil Petition
☐ Partnership and corporate governance (21)
☐ Other petition *(not specified above)* (43)

2. This case ☐ is ☐ is not complex under rule 3.400 of the California Rules of Court. If the case is complex, mark the factors requiring exceptional judicial management:
   a. ☐ Large number of separately represented parties
   b. ☐ Extensive motion practice raising difficult or novel issues that will be time-consuming to resolve
   c. ☐ Substantial amount of documentary evidence
   d. ☐ Large number of witnesses
   e. ☐ Coordination with related actions pending in one or more courts in other counties, states, or countries, or in a federal court
   f. ☐ Substantial postjudgment judicial supervision

3. Remedies sought *(check all that apply):* a. ☐ monetary b. ☐ nonmonetary; declaratory or injunctive relief c. ☐ punitive
4. Number of causes of action *(specify):*
5. This case ☐ is ☐ is not a class action suit.
6. If there are any known related cases, file and serve a notice of related case. *(You may use form CM-015.)*

Date:

▶

_____
(TYPE OR PRINT NAME)

_____
(SIGNATURE OF PARTY OR ATTORNEY FOR PARTY)

NOTICE
- Plaintiff must file this cover sheet with the first paper filed in the action or proceeding (except small claims cases or cases filed under the Probate Code, Family Code, or Welfare and Institutions Code). (Cal. Rules of Court, rule 3.220.) Failure to file may result in sanctions.
- File this cover sheet in addition to any cover sheet required by local court rule.
- If this case is complex under rule 3.400 et seq. of the California Rules of Court, you must serve a copy of this cover sheet on **all** other parties to the action or proceeding.
- Unless this is a collections case under rule 3.740 or a complex case, this cover sheet will be used for statistical purposes only.

Page 1 of 2

Form Adopted for Mandatory Use Judicial Council of California CM-010 [Rev. July 1, 2007]	**CIVIL CASE COVER SHEET**	Cal. Rules of Court, rules 2.30, 3.220, 3.400–3.403, 3.740; Cal. Standards of Judicial Administration, std. 3.10 www.courtinfo.ca.gov

NC-110G

PETITION OF *(Name of petitioner or petitioners)*:	CASE NUMBER:
FOR CHANGE OF NAME	

DECLARATION OF GUARDIAN
Supplemental Attachment to *Petition for Change of Name* (Form NC-100)   Attachment ____ of ____

*(If you are petitioning as a guardian of a minor, you must use a **separate** supplemental attachment for **each minor** whose name is to be changed.)*

7. a. Petitioner *(name)*:

   b. Petitioner's address *(street, city, county, and zip code)*:

   c. Petitioner is the guardian of the following minor whose name is to be changed:
      (1) Name *(present name of child)*:
      (2) Address *(street, city, county, and zip code)*:

   d. Petitioner was appointed guardian of the minor identified in item 7c by *(specify)*:
      (1) Superior Court of California, County of *(name)*:
      (2) Department *(check one)*: ☐ Juvenile   ☐ Probate
      (3) Case number *(specify)*:
      (4) Date of appointment *(specify)*:

   e. The grandparents of the minor whose name is to be changed are *(provide names and addresses, if known)*:
      (1) Grandfather *(name)*:   *(address)*:

      (2) Grandmother *(name)*:   *(address)*:

      (3) Grandfather *(name)*:   *(address)*:

      (4) Grandmother *(name)*:   *(address)*:

   f. The minor identified in item 7c is likely to remain under the guardian's care until the minor reaches the age of majority because *(explain)*:

      ☐ Continued *(if you need additional space, check the box, prepare an Attachment 7f, and attach it to this declaration)*.
   g. The minor identified in item 7c is not likely to be returned to the custody of his or her parents because *(explain)*:

      ☐ Continued *(if you need additional space, check the box, prepare an Attachment 7g, and attach it to this declaration)*.
   h. Other relevant information about the guardianship and why the proposed name change is in the best interest of the minor *(specify)*:

      ☐ Continued *(if you need additional space, check the box, prepare an Attachment 7h, and attach it to this declaration)*.

I declare under penalty of perjury under the laws of the State of California that the information in the foregoing declaration is true and correct.

Date:

▶

_____
(TYPE OR PRINT NAME)

_____
(SIGNATURE OF PETITIONER)

Guardian of *(name of minor)*:

Form Adopted for Mandatory Use
Judicial Council of California
NC-110G [New January 1, 2001]

**SUPPLEMENTAL ATTACHMENT TO
PETITION FOR CHANGE OF NAME**
(Declaration of Guardian)

WEST GROUP
Official Publisher

Code of Civil Procedure, § 1275 et seq.

NC-130G

PETITIONER OR ATTORNEY *(Name, State Bar number, and address)*:

TELEPHONE NO.:   FAX NO. *(Optional)*:

E-MAIL ADDRESS *(Optional)*:

ATTORNEY FOR *(Name)*:

SUPERIOR COURT OF CALIFORNIA, COUNTY OF

    STREET ADDRESS:

    MAILING ADDRESS:

    CITY AND ZIP CODE:

    BRANCH NAME:

PETITION OF *(Name of each petitioner)*:

                               FOR CHANGE OF NAME

DECREE CHANGING NAME OF MINOR (BY GUARDIAN)	CASE NUMBER:

1. The petition was duly considered:

  a. ☐ at the hearing on *(date)*:   in Courtroom: of the above-entitled court.

  b. ☐ without hearing.

THE COURT FINDS

2. a. All notices required by law have been given.

  b. The person whose name is to be changed *(specify present name)*:
    is a minor.

  c. The petition for change of name was filed on behalf of the minor by the minor's guardian *(name)*:

  d. The minor whose name is to be changed is likely to remain in the guardian's care until the age of majority.

  e. The minor whose name is to be changed is not likely to be returned to the custody of his or her parents.

  f. The minor whose name is to be changed

    (1) ☐ is not ☐ is under the jurisdiction of the Department of Corrections, and

    (2) ☐ is not ☐ is required to register as a sex offender under section 290 of the Penal Code.

    These determinations were made ☐ by using CLETS/CJIS ☐ based on information provided to the clerk of the
    court by a local law enforcement agency.

  g. ☐ No objections to the proposed change of name were made.

  h. ☐ Objections to the proposed change of name were made by *(name)*:

  i. It appears to the satisfaction of the court that all the allegations in the petition are true and sufficient, that the proposed name
    change is in the best interest of the minor, and that the petition should be granted.

  j. ☐ Other findings (if any):

THE COURT ORDERS

3. The name of *(present name)*:
  is changed to *(new name)*:

Date: _____

                                                  _____
                                              JUDGE OF THE SUPERIOR COURT

                                   ☐ SIGNATURE OF JUDGE FOLLOWS LAST ATTACHMENT

Form Adopted for Mandatory Use
Judicial Council of California
NC-130G [Rev. July 1, 2007]

DECREE CHANGING NAME
(Change of Name of Minor by Guardian)

Code of Civil Procedure, §§ 1278, 1279

NC-200

PETITIONER OR ATTORNEY *(Name, State Bar number, and address):*

TELEPHONE NO.:   FAX NO. *(Optional):*

E-MAIL ADDRESS *(Optional):*

ATTORNEY FOR *(Name):*

SUPERIOR COURT OF CALIFORNIA, COUNTY OF

STREET ADDRESS:

MAILING ADDRESS:

CITY AND ZIP CODE:

BRANCH NAME:

PETITION OF *(Name):*

PETITION FOR CHANGE OF NAME AND GENDER	CASE NUMBER:

Before you complete this petition, you should read the *Instructions for Filing a Petition* on the next page. You must answer all questions and check all boxes on this petition that apply to you. You must file this petition in the superior court of the county where the person whose name is to be changed resides.

1. Petitioner *(present name):*   is a resident of this county.
   Petitioner requests that the court decree that petitioner's name is changed to *(proposed name):*

2. Petitioner requests a decree that the petitioner's gender is changed:
   (1) ☐ from male to female.
   (2) ☐ from female to male.

3. An affidavit or a declaration of a physician documenting the gender change through surgical treatment as provided under Health and Safety Code sections 103425 and 103430 is attached to this petition. (Declaration of Physician *(form NC-210)* may be used for this purpose.)

4. Petitioner requests that the court order that a new birth certificate be issued reflecting the gender and name changes sought by this petition.

5. Petitioner requests that the court issue an order directing all interested persons to appear and show cause why this petition should not be granted.

6. Petitioner provides the following information in support of this petition:

   a. The information contained in the physician's affidavit or declaration.

   b–f. The information contained in the attachment *(attach a copy of the attachment* Name and Information About the Person Whose Name Is to Be Changed (Attachment to Petition) *(form NC-110)).*

Form Adopted for Mandatory Use
Judicial Council of California
NC-200 [Rev. July 1, 2006]

**PETITION FOR CHANGE OF NAME
AND GENDER**

Code of Civil Procedure §, 1275 et seq.;
Health & Safety Code, §§ 103430, 103435
www.courtinfo.ca.gov

INSTRUCTIONS FOR FILING A PETITION FOR CHANGE OF NAME AND GENDER

1. **Where to File**
   The petition for change of name and gender must be filed in the superior court in the county where the petitioner presently lives.

2. **Whose Name May Be Changed**
   The petition may be used to change one's name and gender.

3. **What Forms Are Required**
   You need an original and two copies of each of the following documents:
   a. *Petition for Change of Name and Gender* (form NC-200)
   b. *Name and Information About the Person Whose Name Is to Be Changed (Attachment to Petition)* (form NC-110)
   c. *Declaration of Physician* (form NC-210) (signed by the physician and attached to form NC-200)
   d. *Order to Show Cause for Change of Name and Gender* (form NC-220)
   e. *Decree Changing Name and Gender* (form NC-230)

4. **Filing and Filing Fee**
   Prepare an original *Civil Case Cover Sheet* (form CM-010). File the original petition and *Civil Case Cover Sheet* with the clerk of the court and obtain two filed-endorsed copies of the petition. A filing fee will be charged unless you qualify for a fee waiver. (If you want to apply for a fee waiver, see *Application for Waiver of Court Fees and Costs* (form 982(a)(17)); *Information Sheet on Waiver of Court Fees and Costs* (form 982(a)(17)(A)–INFO); and *Order on Application for Waiver of Court Fees and Costs* (form 982(a)(18)).)

5. **Requesting a Court Hearing Date**
   You should request a date for the hearing on the *Order to Show Cause* at least six weeks in the future.

6. **Filing the Order to Show Cause**
   After the hearing date has been included and you have obtained a judge's signature on the *Order to Show Cause,* file the original order in the clerk's office and obtain filed-endorsed copies of the order.

7. **Publishing the Order to Show Cause**
   A copy of the *Order to Show Cause* must be published in a local newspaper of general circulation once a week for **at least four consecutive weeks** before the date of the hearing on the petition. The petitioner selects the newspaper from among those newspapers legally qualified to publish orders and notices. The newspaper used must file a Proof of Publication with the superior court before the hearing. If no newspaper of general circulation is published in the county, the court may order the *Order to Show Cause* to be posted by the clerk.

8. **Domestic Violence Confidentiality Program**
   In cases where the petitioner is a participant in the domestic violence confidentiality program, the petition, the order to show cause published in the newspaper, and the decree should, instead of giving the proposed name, indicate that the name is confidential and on file with the Secretary of State.

9. **Court Hearing**
   Bring copies of all documents to the hearing. If the judge grants the name and gender change petition, the judge will sign the original decree.

10. To obtain a new birth certificate reflecting the change of gender, file a certified copy of the order within 30 days with the Secretary of State and the State Registrar and pay the applicable fees. You may write or contact the State Registrar at:

California Department of Health Services
Office of Vital Records
MS 5103, P.O. Box 997410
Sacramento, CA 95899-7410

Phone: (916) 445-2684
Web site: www.dhs.ca.gov

Local courts may supplement these instructions. Check with the court to determine whether supplemental information is available. For instance, the court may provide you with additional written information identifying the department that handles name and gender change petitions, the times when petitions are heard, and the newspapers that may be used to publish the *Order to Show Cause.*

_____ **NC-210/NC-310**

PETITION OF *(Name):*	CASE NUMBER:

Page ____ of ____

**DECLARATION OF PHYSICIAN
DOCUMENTING CHANGE OF GENDER THROUGH SURGICAL TREATMENT
UNDER HEALTH AND SAFETY CODE SECTIONS 103425 AND 103430**

Attachment to *Petition for Change of Name and Gender* (form NC-200) or *Petition for Change of Gender and Issuance of New Birth Certificate* (Form NC-300)

I declare under penalty of perjury under the laws of the State of California that the information in the foregoing declaration is true and correct.

Date:

_____   ▶   _____
(TYPE OR PRINT NAME OF PHYSICIAN)   (SIGNATURE OF PHYSICIAN)

**DECLARATION OF PHYSICIAN—ATTACHMENT TO PETITION
(Change of Name and Gender/Change of Gender)**

NC-220

PETITIONER OR ATTORNEY *(Name, state bar number, and address)*:	**FOR COURT USE ONLY**

TELEPHONE NO.:   FAX NO. *(Optional)*:

E-MAIL ADDRESS *(Optional)*:

ATTORNEY FOR *(Name)*:

SUPERIOR COURT OF CALIFORNIA, COUNTY OF

STREET ADDRESS:

MAILING ADDRESS:

CITY AND ZIP CODE:

BRANCH NAME:

PETITION OF *(Name of petitioner)*:

FOR CHANGE OF NAME AND GENDER

ORDER TO SHOW CAUSE FOR CHANGE OF NAME AND GENDER	CASE NUMBER:

TO ALL INTERESTED PERSONS:

1. Petitioner *(present name)*:   has filed a petition with this court for a decree changing petitioner's name to *(proposed name)*:

2. Petitioner has also filed a petition for a decree changing petitioner's gender ☐ from female to male ☐ from male to female and for the issuance of a new birth certificate reflecting the gender and name changes.

3. THE COURT ORDERS that all persons interested in this matter shall appear before this court at the hearing indicated below to show cause, if any, why the petition should not be granted.

NOTICE OF HEARING

a. Date: Time: ☐ Dept.:   ☐ Room:

b. The address of the court is ☐ same as noted above ☐ other *(specify)*:

4. a. ☐ A copy of this *Order to Show Cause* shall be published at least once each week for four successive weeks prior to the date set for hearing on the petition in the following newspaper of general circulation, printed in this county *(specify newspaper)*:

b. ☐ Other *(specify)*:

Date:

_____
JUDGE OF THE SUPERIOR COURT

Form Adopted for Mandatory Use Judicial Council of California NC-220 [New January 1, 2003]	**ORDER TO SHOW CAUSE** **FOR CHANGE OF NAME AND GENDER**	Code of Civ. Proc.,§ 1275 et seq.; Health & Safety Code, §§ 103430, 103435

NC-230

PETITIONER OR ATTORNEY *(Name, state bar number, and address):*

FOR COURT USE ONLY

TELEPHONE NO.:   FAX NO. *(Optional):*

E-MAIL ADDRESS *(Optional):*

ATTORNEY FOR *(Name):*

SUPERIOR COURT OF CALIFORNIA, COUNTY OF
    STREET ADDRESS:
    MAILING ADDRESS:
    CITY AND ZIP CODE:
    BRANCH NAME:

PETITION OF *(Name of petitioner):*

FOR CHANGE OF NAME AND GENDER

DECREE CHANGING NAME AND GENDER

CASE NUMBER:

1. The petition came regularly for hearing on *(date):*   in Courtroom: of the above-entitled court.

THE COURT FINDS

2. a. All notices required by law have been given.
  b. Each person whose name is to be changed identified in item 3 below
    (1) ☐ is not ☐ is   under the jurisdiction of the Department of Corrections, and
    (2) ☐ is not ☐ is   required to register as a sex offender under section 290 of the Penal Code.
    These determinations were made ☐ by using CLETS/CJIS ☐ based on information provided to the clerk of the
    court by a local law enforcement agency.
  c. ☐ No objections to the proposed change of name were made.
  d. ☐ Objections to the proposed change of name were made by *(name):*

  e. It appears to the satisfaction of the court that all the allegations in the petition are true and sufficient and that the petition should
    be granted.
  f. ☐ Other findings *(if any):*

THE COURT ORDERS

3. The name of *(present name):*
  is changed to *(new name):*

THE COURT FURTHER ORDERS

4. The gender of *(new name):*
  is changed:
  a. ☐ from male to female.
  b. ☐ from female to male.

THE COURT FURTHER ORDERS

5. A new birth certificate shall be issued reflecting the changes in name and gender.

Date: _____

_____
JUDGE OF THE SUPERIOR COURT
☐ SIGNATURE OF JUDGE FOLLOWS LAST ATTACHMENT

Page 1 of 1

Form Adopted for Mandatory Use
Judicial Council of California
NC-230 [New January 1, 2003]

DECREE CHANGING NAME AND GENDER

Code of Civil Procedure, §§ 1278, 1279;
Health & Safety Code, §§ 103430, 103435

A Public Service Agency

MEDICAL CERTIFICATION AND AUTHORIZATION
(Gender Change)

SECTION 1 – APPLICANT'S TRUE FULL NAME (TO BE COMPLETED BY THE APPLICANT)

LAST	FIRST	MIDDLE	DATE OF BIRTH *(MM,DD,YYYY)*

MAILING ADDRESS	CITY	STATE	ZIP CODE	CALIFORNIA DRIVER LICENSE/IDENTIFICATION CARD NUMBER

RESIDENCE ADDRESS *(IF DIFFERENT FROM MAILING ADDRESS)*	CITY	STATE	ZIP CODE

DAYTIME TELEPHONE NUMBER	SOCIAL SECURITY NUMBER
( )	

SECTION 2 – CERTIFICATION

I certify (or declare) under penalty of perjury under the laws of the State of California that the foregoing is true and correct.

APPLICANT SIGNATURE	DATE
X	

AUTHORIZATION

All records of the department relating to the physical or mental condition of any person are confidential and not open to public inspection per California Vehicle Code Section 1808.5.

I hereby authorize my physician/psychologist, or health service provider, to release the information below to the California Department of Motor Vehicles for the purpose of obtaining a driver license or an identification card under my preferred gender. _____ (Applicant's Initials)

SECTION 3 – TO BE COMPLETED BY A PHYSICIAN/PSYCHOLOGIST LICENSED IN THE UNITED STATES

My professional opinion is that the applicant's:

Gender identification is: ☐ Male ☐ Female

Demeanor is: ☐ Male ☐ Female

Only a physician licensed in the United States can certify that gender identification is complete.

Gender identification is: ☐ Complete ☐ Transitional

SECTION 4 – TO BE COMPLETED BY A PHYSICIAN/PSYCHOLOGIST LICENSED IN THE UNITED STATES

FULL NAME OF PHYSICIAN/PSYCHOLOGIST *(PRINT)*

☐ Physician ☐ Psychologist	EXAMINATION DATE	MEDICAL CASE NUMBER
EMAIL ADDRESS		

MEDICAL LICENSE OR CERTIFICATE NUMBER	ISSUING STATE	TELEPHONE NUMBER
		( )

NAME OF HOSPITAL OR MEDICAL CLINIC

MAILING ADDRESS	CITY	STATE	ZIP CODE

PHYSICAL ADDRESS *(IF DIFFERENT FROM MAILING ADDRESS)*	CITY	STATE	ZIP CODE

SECTION 5 – CERTIFICATION

I certify (or declare) under penalty of perjury under the laws of the State of California that the foregoing is true and correct.

SIGNATURE OF PHYSICIAN OR PSYCHOLOGIST	DATE
X	

SECTION 6 – FOR DMV USE ONLY

DMV MANAGER OR DESIGNEE'S SIGNATURE:	DATE LINE STAMP
X	

This form is void five (5) years from the date of the physician or psychologist certification.

DL 329 (NEW 8/2008) WWW

INSTRUCTIONS FOR COMPLETING THE
MEDICAL CERTIFICATION AND AUTHORIZATION
(Gender Change)

SECTION 1

This section is to be completed by the applicant and must include all required information.

This form cannot be used to establish True Full Name or make a name change. *To establish True Full Name or make a name change, you must submit an approved document identified in California Code of Regulations, Title XIII, Article 2, Sections 15.00 and 20.04. The list of approved documents is also available at **www.dmv.ca.gov** and the Department of Motor Vehicles Fast Facts brochure for Birth Date/Legal Presence and True Full Name.*

SECTION 2

This section is to be signed and dated by the applicant.

SECTION 3

This section must be completed by a physician or psychologist licensed in the United States. Either a physician or psychologist can certify that gender identification is transitional or incomplete.

Only a physician can certify that gender identification is complete.

SECTION 4

This section must be completed by a physician or psychologist licensed in the United States.

Only a physician can certify that gender identification is complete.

SECTION 5

This section is to be signed and dated by the physician or psychologist.

SECTION 6

This section is for the California Department of Motor Vehicles (DMV) use only.

Failure to complete all required sections of the Medical Certification and Authorization (Gender Change) form will result in refusal of the Driver License or Identification Card Application (DL 44) and the refusal of a driver license or identification card with requested gender identity.

For further questions or assistance, please call DMV's Record Security and Identification Unit, (916) 657-6613.

This form is void five (5) years from the date of the physician or psychologist certification.

DL 329 (NEW 8/2008) WWW

NC-300

ATTORNEY OR PARTY WITHOUT ATTORNEY *(Name, State Bar number, and address):*

TELEPHONE NO.:   FAX NO. *(Optional):*
E-MAIL ADDRESS *(Optional):*
ATTORNEY FOR *(Name):*

SUPERIOR COURT OF CALIFORNIA, COUNTY OF
    STREET ADDRESS:
    MAILING ADDRESS:
    CITY AND ZIP CODE:
    BRANCH NAME:

PETITION OF *(Name):*

PETITION FOR CHANGE OF GENDER AND ISSUANCE OF NEW BIRTH CERTIFICATE	CASE NUMBER:

1. Petitioner *(name):*

    is a resident of the county where this petition is filed.

2. Petitioner requests an order for the issuance of a new birth certificate reflecting the change of petitioner's gender

    a. ☐ from male to female.

    b. ☐ from female to male.

3. A declaration by a physician documenting the gender change through surgical treatment as provided under Health and Safety Code sections 103425 and 103430 is filed with this petition. *(Attach a copy of Declaration of Physician—Attachment to Petition (form NC-310).)*

4. Petitioner ☐ has ☐ has not already obtained a decree of change of name. *(If petitioner has obtained a decree of change of name, attach a certified copy of the decree to this petition.)*

5. Petitioner requests that the court issue an order setting a hearing on this petition at which objections may be filed by any person who can show to the court good reason against the change of birth certificate.

I declare under penalty of perjury under the laws of the State of California that the information above is true and correct.

Date:

_____
(TYPE OR PRINT NAME OF PETITIONER)

▶ _____
(SIGNATURE OF PETITIONER)

Page 1 of 2

PETITION FOR CHANGE OF GENDER AND ISSUANCE OF NEW BIRTH CERTIFICATE

Health & Safety Code, §§ 103425, 103430,
103435, 103440
www.courtinfo.ca.gov

INSTRUCTIONS FOR FILING PETITION FOR CHANGE OF GENDER
AND ISSUANCE OF NEW BIRTH CERTIFICATE

(This instruction page is for the information of petitioners. It is not part of the petition and does not need to be filed.)

1. Where to File

The petition for the issuance of a new birth certificate reflecting a change in gender must be filed in the superior court in the county where the petitioner presently lives.

2. What Forms Are Required

You will need an original and a copy of each of the following documents:

a. *Petition for Change of Gender and Issuance of New Birth Certificate* (form NC-300).

b. *Declaration of Physician—Attachment to Petition* (form NC-310) (signed by the physician and attached to form NC-300).

c. *Notice of Hearing on Petition for Change of Gender and Issuance of New Birth Certificate* (form NC-320).

d. *Order for Change of Gender and Issuance of New Birth Certificate* (form NC-330).

In addition, if you have already obtained a decree of change of name, attach a certified copy of the decree to the petition.

3. Filing Fee

Prepare an original *Civil Case Cover Sheet* (form CM-010). File the original petition and *Civil Case Cover Sheet* with the clerk of the court and obtain a filed-endorsed copy of the petition. A filing fee will be charged unless you qualify for a fee waiver. (If you want to apply for a fee waiver, see *Application for Waiver of Court Fees and Costs* (form 982(a)(17)); *Information Sheet on Waiver of Court Fees and Costs* (form 982(a)(17)(A)–INFO); and *Order on Application for Waiver of Court Fees and Costs* (form 982(a)(18)).

4. Requesting a Court Hearing Date

You should request a date for the hearing on the *Notice of Hearing on Petition for Change of Gender and Issuance of New Birth Certificate* (form NC-320).

5. Filing the Order to Show Cause

Take the completed form to the clerk's office. The clerk will provide the hearing date and location, obtain the judicial officer's signature, file the original, and give you a copy.

6. Court Hearing

Bring copies of all documents to the hearing. If the judge grants the petition, the judge will sign the *Order for Change of Gender and Issuance of New Birth Certificate* (form NC-300).

7. New Birth Certificate

To obtain a new birth certificate reflecting the change of gender, file a certified copy of the order within 30 days with the Secretary of State and the State Registrar and pay the applicable fees. You may write or contact the State Registrar at:

California Department of Health Services
Office of Vital Records
MS 5103, P.O. Box 997410
Sacramento, CA 95899-7410

Phone: (916) 445-2684
Web site: www.dhs.ca.gov

Local courts may supplement these instructions. Check with the court to determine whether supplemental information is available. For instance, the court may provide you with additional written information identifying the department that handles these petitions and the times when petitions are heard.

NC-300 [New July 1, 2006]　　**PETITION FOR CHANGE OF GENDER AND ISSUANCE**　　Page 2 of 2
OF NEW BIRTH CERTIFICATE

NC-320

ATTORNEY OR PARTY WITHOUT ATTORNEY *(Name, State Bar number, and address)*:

TELEPHONE NO.:   FAX NO. *(Optional)*:
E-MAIL ADDRESS *(Optional)*:
ATTORNEY FOR *(Name)*:

SUPERIOR COURT OF CALIFORNIA, COUNTY OF
   STREET ADDRESS:
   MAILING ADDRESS:
   CITY AND ZIP CODE:
   BRANCH NAME:

PETITION OF *(Name)*:

NOTICE OF HEARING ON PETITION FOR CHANGE OF GENDER AND ISSUANCE OF NEW BIRTH CERTIFICATE	CASE NUMBER:

NOTICE:

1. Petitioner *(name)*:   is a resident of this county.

2. Petitioner has filed a petition requesting an order for the issuance of a new birth certificate reflecting the change of petitioner's gender

   a. ☐ from male to female.
   b. ☐ from female to male.

3. **THE COURT ORDERS** that any person who can show good reason against the change of birth certificate requested in the petition may appear before this court at the hearing indicated below to file objections.

NOTICE OF HEARING

   a. Date: Time: Dept.:   Room:

   b. The address of the court is ☐ same as noted above ☐ other *(specify)*:

4. ☐ Other orders *(specify)*:

Date: ▶ _____
                                       JUDICIAL OFFICER

Form Approved for Optional Use
Judicial Council of California
NC-320 [New July 1, 2006]

NOTICE OF HEARING ON PETITION FOR CHANGE OF GENDER AND ISSUANCE OF NEW BIRTH CERTIFICATE

Health & Safety Code, §§ 103425, 103430, 103435, 103440
www.courtinfo.ca.gov

NC-330

ATTORNEY OR PARTY WITHOUT ATTORNEY *(Name, State Bar number, and address):*

TELEPHONE NO.:   FAX NO. *(Optional):*

E-MAIL ADDRESS *(Optional):*

ATTORNEY FOR *(Name):*

SUPERIOR COURT OF CALIFORNIA, COUNTY OF

STREET ADDRESS:

MAILING ADDRESS:

CITY AND ZIP CODE:

BRANCH NAME:

PETITION OF *(Name):*

ORDER FOR CHANGE OF GENDER AND ISSUANCE OF NEW BIRTH CERTIFICATE	CASE NUMBER:

1. The petition of *(name):*   for issuance of a new birth certificate
reflecting a change of gender came on regularly for hearing on *(date):*

THE COURT FINDS

2. a. ☐ No objections to the proposed change of gender were made.

    b. ☐ Objections to the proposed change of gender were made by *(name):*

    c. It appears to the satisfaction of the court that all the allegations in the petition are true and sufficient and that the petition should be granted.

    d. ☐ Other findings *(if any):*

THE COURT ORDERS

3. The gender of the petitioner has been changed

    a. ☐ from male to female.

    b. ☐ from female to male.

THE COURT FURTHER ORDERS

4. A new birth certificate reflecting the change of gender described in item 3 shall be issued.

5. A certified copy of this order shall be filed within 30 days with the Secretary of State and the State Registrar. When the State Registrar receives a certified copy of this order and payment of the applicable fees, the State Registrar shall establish for the petitioner a new birth certificate reflecting the gender of the petitioner as it has been altered.

Date: _____ ▶ _____

                                                  JUDICIAL OFFICER

Page 1 of 1

Form Approved for Optional Use
Judicial Council of California
NC-330 [New July 1, 2008]

ORDER FOR CHANGE OF GENDER AND ISSUANCE OF NEW BIRTH CERTIFICATE

Health & Safety Code, §§ 103425, 103430, 103435, 103440
www.courtinfo.ca.gov

FW-001-INFO

INFORMATION SHEET ON WAIVER OF SUPERIOR COURT FEES AND COSTS

If you have been sued or if you wish to sue someone, or if you are filing or have received a family law petition, and if you cannot afford to pay court fees and costs, you may not have to pay them in order to go to court. If you are getting public benefits, are a low-income person, or do not have enough income to pay for your household's basic needs *and* your court fees, you may ask the court to waive all or part of your court fees.

1. To make a request to the court to waive your fees in superior court, complete the *Request to Waive Court Fees* (form FW-001). If you qualify, the court will waive all or part of its fees for the following:
   - Filing papers in superior court (other than for an appeal in a case with a value of over $25,000)
   - Making and certifying copies
   - Sheriff's fee to give notice
   - Court fees for telephone hearings
   - Giving notice and certificates
   - Sending papers to another court department
   - Having a court-appointed interpreter in small claims court
   - Reporter's daily fee *(for up to 60 days after the grant of the fee waiver, at the court-approved daily rate)*
   - Preparing, certifying, copying, and sending the clerk's transcript on appeal.

2. You may ask the court to waive other court fees during your case in superior court as well. To do that, complete a *Request to Waive Additional Court Fees (Superior Court)* (form FW-002). The court will consider waiving fees for items such as the following, or other court services you need for your case:
   - Jury fees and expenses
   - Fees for court-appointed experts
   - Reporter's daily fees (*beyond the 60-day period after the grant of the fee waiver, at the court-approved daily rate*)
   - Fees for a peace officer to testify in court
   - Court-appointed interpreter fees for a witness
   - Other necessary court fees

3. If you want the Appellate Division of Superior Court or the Court of Appeal to review an order or judgment against you and you want the court fees waived, ask for and follow the instructions on *Information Sheet on Waiver of Appellate Court Fees, Supreme Court, Court of Appeal, Appellate Division* (form APP-015/FW-015-INFO).

IMPORTANT INFORMATION!

• **You are signing your request under penalty of perjury. Please answer truthfully, accurately, and completely.**

• **The court may ask you for information and evidence.** You may be ordered to go to court to answer questions about your ability to pay court fees and costs and to provide proof of eligibility. Any initial fee waiver you are granted may be ended if you do not go to court when asked. You may be ordered to repay amounts that were waived if the court finds you were not eligible for the fee waiver.

• **If you receive a fee waiver, you must tell the court if there is a change in your finances.** You must tell the court within five days if your finances improve or if you become able to pay court fees or costs during this case. (File *Notice to Court of Improved Financial Situation or Settlement* (form FW-010) with the court.) You may be ordered to repay any amounts that were waived after your eligibility came to an end.

• **If you receive a judgment or support order in a family law matter:** You may be ordered to pay all or part of your waived fees and costs if the court finds your circumstances have changed so that you can afford to pay. You will have the opportunity to ask the court for a hearing if the court makes such a decision.

• **If you win your case in the trial court:** In most circumstances the other side will be ordered to pay your waived fees and costs to the court. The court will not enter a satisfaction of judgment until the court is paid. (This does not apply in unlawful detainer cases. Special rules apply in family law cases. (Government Code, section 68637(d), (e).)

• **If you settle your civil case for $10,000 or more:** Any trial court waived fees and costs must first be paid to the court out of the settlement. **The court will have a lien on the settlement in the amount of the waived fees and costs.** The court may refuse to dismiss the case until the lien is satisfied. A request to dismiss the case (use form CIV-110) must have a declaration under penalty of perjury that the waived fees and costs have been paid. Special rules apply to family law cases.

• **The court can collect fees and costs due to the court.** If waived fees and costs are ordered paid to the trial court, the court can start collection proceedings and add a $25 fee plus any additional costs of collection to the other fees and costs owed to the court.

• **The fee waiver ends.** The fee waiver expires 60 days after the judgment, dismissal, or other final disposition of the case or earlier if a court finds that you are not eligible for a fee waiver.

• **If you are in jail or state prison:** Prisoners may be required to pay the full cost of the filing fee in the trial court but may be allowed to do so over time.

Judicial Council of California, www.courtinfo.ca.gov
Revised July 1, 2009
Government Code, §§ 68630–68640
California Rules of Court, rule 3.51

**Information Sheet on Waiver of
Superior Court Fees and Costs**

FW-001-INFO, Page 1 of 1

American LegalNet, Inc.
www.FormsWorkflow.com

FW-001 — Request to Waive Court Fees

CONFIDENTIAL

Clerk stamps date here when form is filed.

If you are getting public benefits, are a low-income person, or do not have enough income to pay for household's basic needs and your court fees, you may use this form to ask the court to waive all or part of your court fees. The court may order you to answer questions about your finances. If the court waives the fees, you may still have to pay later if:

- You cannot give the court proof of your eligibility,
- Your financial situation improves during this case, or
- You settle your civil case for **$10,000** or more. The trial court that waives your fees will have a lien on any such settlement in the amount of the waived fees and costs. The court may also charge you any collection costs.

Fill in court name and street address:

1. **Your Information** *(person asking the court to waive the fees):*
   Name: _____
   Street or mailing address: _____
   City: _____ State: _____ Zip: _____
   Phone number: _____

Fill in case number and name:

Case Number:

2. **Your Job,** if you have one *(job title):* _____
   Name of employer: _____
   Employer's address: _____

Case Name:

3. **Your lawyer,** if you have one *(name, firm or affiliation, address, phone number, and State Bar number):*
   _____

   a. The lawyer has agreed to advance all or a portion of your fees or costs *(check one):* Yes ☐ No ☐
   b. *(If yes, your lawyer must sign here)* Lawyer's signature: _____
      If your lawyer is not providing legal-aid type services based on your low income, you may have to go to a hearing to explain why you are asking the court to waive the fees.

4. **What court's fees or costs are you asking to be waived?**
   ☑ Superior Court (See *Information Sheet on Waiver of Superior Court Fees and Costs* (form FW-001-INFO).)
   ☐ Supreme Court, Court of Appeal, or Appellate Division of Superior Court (See *Information Sheet on Waiver of Appellate Court Fees and Costs* (form APP-015/FW-015-INFO).)

5. **Why are you asking the court to waive your court fees?**
   a. ☐ I receive *(check all that apply):* ☐ Medi-Cal ☐ Food Stamps ☐ SSI ☐ SSP ☐ County Relief/General Assistance ☐ IHSS (In-Home Supportive Services) ☐ CalWORKS or Tribal TANF (Tribal Temporary Assistance for Needy Families) ☐ CAPI (Cash Assistance Program for Aged, Blind and Disabled)
   b. ☐ My gross monthly household income (before deductions for taxes) is less than the amount listed below. *(If you check 5b you must fill out 7, 8 and 9 on page 2 of this form.)*

Family Size	Family Income	Family Size	Family Income	Family Size	Family Income	
1	$1,128.13	3	$1,907.30	5	$2,686.46	*If more than 6 people at home, add $389.59 for each extra person.*
2	$1,517.71	4	$2,296.88	6	$3,076.05	

   c. ☐ I do not have enough income to pay for my household's basic needs *and* the court fees. I ask the court to *(check one):* ☐ waive all court fees ☐ waive some of the court fees ☐ let me make payments over time *(Explain):* _____ *(If you check 5c, you must fill out page 2.)*

6. ☐ Check here if you asked the court to waive your court fees for this case in the last six months.
   (If your previous request is reasonably available, please attach it to this form and check here: ☐)

I declare under penalty of perjury under the laws of the State of California that the information I have provided on this form and all attachments is true and correct.

Date: _____

▶ _____

_____
Print your name here

_____
Sign here

Judicial Council of California, *www.courtinfo.ca.gov*
Revised July 2, 2009, Mandatory Form
Government Code, § 68633
Cal. Rules of Court, rules 3.51, 8.26, and 8.818

Request to Waive Court Fees

FW-001, Page 1 of 2

Case Number:

Your name: _____

*If you checked 5a on page 1, do not fill out below. If you checked 5b, fill out questions 7, 8, and 9 only. If you checked 5c, you **must** fill out this entire page. If you need more space, attach form MC-025 or attach a sheet of paper and write Financial Information and your name and case number at the top.*

(7) ☐ Check here if your income changes a lot from month to month. Fill out below based on your average income for the past 12 months.

(8) **Your Monthly Income**

a. Gross monthly income (before deductions): $ _____
List each payroll deduction and amount below:
(1) _____ $ _____
(2) _____ $ _____
(3) _____ $ _____
(4) _____ $ _____

b. Total deductions (add 8a (1)-(4) above): $ _____

c. Total monthly take-home pay (8a minus 8b): $ _____

d. List the source and amount of *any* other income you get each month, including: spousal/child support, retirement, social security, disability, unemployment, military basic allowance for quarters (BAQ), veterans payments, dividends, interest, trust income, annuities, net business or rental income, reimbursement for job-related expenses, gambling or lottery winnings, etc.
(1) _____ $ _____
(2) _____ $ _____
(3) _____ $ _____
(4) _____ $ _____

e. **Your total monthly income is** (8c plus 8d): $ _____

(9) **Household Income**

a. List all other persons living in your home and their income; include only your spouse and all individuals who depend in whole or in part on you for support, or on whom you depend in whole or in part for support.

Name	Age	Relationship	Gross Monthly Income
(1)			$
(2)			$
(3)			$
(4)			$

b. **Total monthly income of persons above:** $ _____

Total monthly income and household income (8e plus 9b): $ _____

To list any other facts you want the court to know, such as unusual medical expenses, family emergencies, etc., attach form MC-025. Or attach a sheet of paper, and write Financial Information and your name and case number at the top. Check here if you attach another page. ☐

Important! **If your financial situation or ability to pay court fees improves, you must notify the court within five days on form FW-010.**

(10) **Your Money and Property**

a. Cash - $ _____

b. All financial accounts (List bank name and amount):
(1) _____ $ _____
(2) _____ $ _____
(3) _____ $ _____
(4) _____ $ _____

c. Cars, boats, and other vehicles

Make / Year	Fair Market Value	How Much You Still Owe
(1)	$	$
(2)	$	$
(3)	$	$

d. Real estate

Address	Fair Market Value	How Much You Still Owe
(1)	$	$
(2)	$	$
(3)	$	$

e. Other personal property (jewelry, furniture, furs, stocks, bonds, etc.):

Describe	Fair Market Value	How Much You Still Owe
(1)	$	$
(2)	$	$
(3)	$	$

(11) **Your Monthly Expenses**
(Do not include payroll deductions you already listed in 8b.)

a. Rent or house payment & maintenance $ _____
b. Food and household supplies $ _____
c. Utilities and telephone $ _____
d. Clothing $ _____
e. Laundry and cleaning $ _____
f. Medical and dental expenses $ _____
g. Insurance (life, health, accident, etc.) $ _____
h. School, child care $ _____
i. Child, spousal support (another marriage) $ _____
j. Transportation, gas, auto repair and insurance $ _____
k. Installment payments (list each below):
Paid to:
(1) _____ $ _____
(2) _____ $ _____
(3) _____ $ _____

l. Wages/earnings withheld by court order $ _____
m. Any other monthly expenses (list each below):
Paid to: How Much?
(1) _____ $ _____
(2) _____ $ _____
(3) _____ $ _____

Total monthly expenses (add 11a –11m above): $ _____

Request to Waive Court Fees

FW-001, Page 2 of 2

MC–025

SHORT TITLE:

CASE NUMBER:

ATTACHMENT *(Number):* _____   **Page** _____ of _____

(This Attachment may be used with any Judicial Council form.)   *(Add pages as required)*

1
2
3
4
5
6
7
8
9
10
11
12
13
14
15
16
17
18
19
20
21
22
23
24
25
26
27   *(If the item that this Attachment concerns is made under penalty of perjury, all statements in this Attachment are made under penalty of perjury.)*

Page 1 of 1

Form Approved for Optional Use
Judicial Council of California
MC-025 [Rev. January 1, 2007]

ATTACHMENT
to Judicial Council Form

www.courtinfo.ca.gov

FW-003

Order on Court Fee Waiver
(Superior Court)

Clerk stamps date here when form is filed.

(1) Person who asked the court to waive court fees:

Name: _____

Street or mailing address: _____

City: _____ State: _____ Zip: _____

(2) Lawyer, if person in (1) has one *(name, address, phone number, e-mail, and State Bar number):* _____

_____

_____

Fill in court name and street address:

Superior Court of California, County of

(3) A request to waive court fees was filed
on *(date):* _____

☐ The court made a previous fee waiver order in this case
on *(date):* _____

Read this form carefully. All checked boxes ☑ are court orders.

Fill in case number and case name:

Case Number:

Case Name:

Notice: The court may order you to answer questions about your finances and later order you to pay back the waived fees. If this happens and you do not pay, the court can make you pay the fees and also charge you collection fees. If there is a change in your financial circumstances during this case that increases your ability to pay fees and costs, you must notify the trial court within five days. (Use form FW-010.) If you win your case, the trial court may order the other side to pay the fees. If you settle your civil case for **$10,000** or more, the trial court will have a lien on the settlement in the amount of the waived fees. The trial court may not dismiss the case until the lien is paid.

(4) After reviewing your *(check one):* ☐ *Request to Waive Court Fees* ☐ *Request to Waive Additional Court Fees*
the court makes the following orders:

a. ☐ The court **grants** your request, as follows:

(1) ☐ **Fee Waiver.** The court grants your request and waives your court fees and costs listed below. *(Cal. Rules of Court, rule 3.55.)* You do not have to pay the court fees for the following:
  • Filing papers in Superior Court
  • Making copies and certifying copies
  • Sheriff's fee to give notice
  • Reporter's daily fee *(for up to 60 days following the fee waiver order at the court-approved daily rate)*
  • Preparing and certifying the clerk's transcript on appeal
  • Giving notice and certificates
  • Sending papers to another court department
  • Court-appointed interpreter in small claims court
  • Court fees for phone hearings

(2) ☐ **Additional Fee Waiver.** The court grants your request and waives your additional superior court fees and costs that are checked below. *(Cal. Rules of Court, rule 3.56.)* You do not have to pay for the checked items.
  ☐ Jury fees and expenses
  ☐ Fees for court-appointed experts
  ☐ Reporter's daily fees *(beyond the 60-day period following the fee waiver order)*
  ☐ Other *(specify):* _____
  ☐ Fees for a peace officer to testify in court
  ☐ Court-appointed interpreter fees for a witness

(3) ☐ **Fee Waiver for Appeal.** The court grants your request and waives the fees and costs checked below, for your appeal. *(Cal. Rules of Court, rules 3.55, 3.56, 8.26, and 8.818.)* You do not have to pay for the checked items.
  ☐ Preparing and certifying clerk's transcript for appeal
  ☐ Other *(specify):* _____

Judicial Council of California, www.courtinfo.ca.gov
Revised July 1, 2009, Mandatory Form
Government Code, § 68634(e)
California Rules of Court, rule 3.52

Order on Court Fee Waiver (Superior Court)

FW-003, Page 1 of 2

Your name: _____

Case Number: _____

b. ☐ The court **denies** your request, as follows:

> **Warning!** If you miss the deadline below, the court cannot process your request for hearing or the court papers you filed with your original request. If the papers were a notice of appeal, the appeal may be dismissed.

(1) ☐ The court **denies** your request because it is incomplete. You have **10 days** after the clerk gives notice of this order (see date below) to:
- Pay your fees and costs, or
- File a new revised request that includes the items listed below *(specify incomplete items):*
_____

(2) ☐ The court **denies** your request because the information you provided on the request shows that you are not eligible for the fee waiver you requested *(specify reasons):* _____

The court has enclosed a blank *Request for Hearing About Court Fee Waiver Order (Superior Court)*, form FW-006. You have **10 days** after the clerk gives notice of this order (see date below) to:
- Pay your fees and costs, or
- Ask for a hearing in order to show the court more information. *(Use form FW-006 to request hearing.)*

c. ☐ The court needs more information to decide whether to grant your request. You must go to court on the date below. The hearing will be about *(specify questions regarding eligibility):* _____
_____

☐ Bring the following proof to support your request if reasonably available:_____

Hearing Date →
Date: _____ Time: _____
Dept.: _____ Rm.: _____

Name and address of court if different from page 1:
_____
_____

> **Warning!** If item c is checked, and you do not go to court on your hearing date, the judge will deny your request to waive court fees, and you will have 10 days to pay your fees. If you miss that deadline, the court cannot process the court papers you filed with your request. If the papers were a notice of appeal, the appeal may be dismissed.

Date: _____

Signature of *(check one):* ☐ *Judicial Officer* ☐ *Clerk, Deputy*

Request for Accommodations. Assistive listening systems, computer-assisted real-time captioning, or sign language interpreter services are available if you ask at least 5 days before your hearing. Contact the clerk's office for *Request for Accommodation*, Form MC-410. (Civil Code, § 54.8.)

Clerk's Certificate of Service

I certify that I am not involved in this case and *(check one):* ☐ A certificate of mailing is attached.

☐ I handed a copy of this order to the party and attorney, if any, listed in ① and ②, at the court, on the date below.

☐ This order was mailed first class, postage paid, to the party and attorney, if any, at the addresses listed in ① and ②, from *(city):* _____, California on the date below.

Date: _____ Clerk, by _____, Deputy

Revised July 1, 2009

This is a Court Order.

FW-003, Page 2 of 2

Order on Court Fee Waiver (Superior Court)

FW-006

Request for Hearing About Court Fee Waiver Order (Superior Court)

CONFIDENTIAL

Clerk stamps date here when form is filed.

(1) Your Information *(person who asked the court to waive court fees):*

Name: _____

Street or mailing address: _____

City: _____ State: _____ Zip: _____

Phone number: _____

(2) Your lawyer, if you have one *(name, address, phone number, e-mail, and State Bar number):* _____

_____

_____

Fill in court name and street address:

Superior Court of California, County of

(3) Date of order denying your request to waive court fees *(month/day/year):* _____

☐ *(Check here if you have a copy of the order denying your request, and attach it to this form.)*

Fill in case number and case name:

Case Number:

Case Name:

(4) I ask the court for a hearing on my fee waiver request so that I can bring more information about my financial situation.

(5) ☐ The additional facts that support my request for a fee waiver are *(describe):*
(Use this space if you want to tell the court in advance what facts you want considered at the hearing. If the space below is not enough, attach form MC-025. Or attach a sheet of paper and write Additional Facts and your name and case number at the top. You may also attach copies of documents you want the court to look at.)

_____

_____

_____

_____

_____

_____

_____

Date: _____

▶ _____

Print your name here

Request for Accommodations. Assistive listening systems, computer-assisted real-time captioning, or sign language interpreter services are available if you ask at least five days before your hearing. Contact the clerk's office for *Request for Accommodation,* form MC-410.

Judicial Council of California, *www.courtinfo.ca.gov*
New July 1, 2009, Mandatory Form
Government Code, § 68634(e)(3)

Request for Hearing About Court Fee Waiver Order (Superior Court)

FW-006, Page 1 of 1

FW-008

Order on Court Fee Waiver
After Hearing (Superior Court)

Clerk stamps date here when form is filed.

(1) **Person who asked the court to waive court fees:**

Name: _____

Street or mailing address: _____

City: _____ State: _____ Zip: _____

(2) **Lawyer, if person in (1) has one** *(name, address, phone number,*

e-mail, and State Bar number): _____

_____

_____

Fill in court name and street address:

Superior Court of California, County of

(3) A request to waive court fees was filed *(date):* _____

(4) There was a hearing on *(date):* _____

at *(time):* _____ in *(Department):* _____

The following people were at the hearing *(check all that apply):*

☐ Person in (1)   ☐ Lawyer in (2)

☐ Others *(names):* _____

_____

Read this form carefully. All checked boxes ☑ are court orders.

Fill in case number and name:

Case Number:

Case Name:

Notice: The court may order you to answer questions about your finances and later order you to pay back the waived fees. If this happens and you do not pay, the court can make you pay the fees and also charge you collection fees. If there is a change in your financial circumstances during this case that increases your ability to pay fees and costs, you must notify the trial court within five days. (Use form FW-010.) If you win your case, the trial court may order the other side to pay the fees. If you settle your civil case for **$10,000** or more, the trial court will have a lien on the settlement in the amount of the waived fees. The trial court may not dismiss the case until the lien is paid.

(5) After reviewing your *(check one):* ☐ *Request to Waive Court Fees* ☐ *Request to Waive Additional Court Fees* **the court makes the following order:**

a. ☐ The court **grants** your request and waives your court fees and costs as follows:

   (1) ☐ **Fee Waiver.** The court **grants** your request and waives your court fees and costs listed below *(Cal. Rules of Court, rule 3.55.)* You do not have to pay the court fees for the following:
   - Filing papers in superior court
   - Making copies and certifying copies
   - Sheriff's fee to give notice
   - Reporter's daily fee *(for up to 60 days after the grant of the fee waiver, at the court-approved daily rate)*
   - Preparing and certifying the clerk's transcript on appeal
   - Giving notice and certificates
   - Sending papers to another court department
   - Court-appointed interpreter in small claims court
   - Court fees for phone hearing

   (2) ☐ **Additional Fee Waiver.** The court **grants** your request and waives your additional superior court fees and costs that are checked below. *(Cal. Rules of Court, rule 3.56.)* You do not have to pay for the checked items.
   - ☐ Jury fees and expenses
   - ☐ Fees for court-appointed experts
   - ☐ Reporter's daily fees *(beyond the 60-day period after grant of the fee waiver, at court-approved daily rate)*
   - ☐ Other *(specify):* _____
   - ☐ Fees for a peace officer to testify in court
   - ☐ Court-appointed interpreter fees for a witness

   (3) ☐ **Fee Waiver for Appeal.** The court **grants** your request and waives the fees and costs checked below, for your appeal. *(Cal. Rules of Court, rules 8.26 and 8.818.)* You do not have to pay for the checked items.
   - ☐ Preparing and certifying clerk's transcript for appeal
   - ☐ Other *(specify):* _____

Judicial Council of California, www.courtinfo.ca.gov
Rev. January 1, 2010, Mandatory Form
Government Code, § 68634(e)
Cal. Rules of Court, rule 3.52

**Order on Court Fee Waiver
After Hearing (Superior Court)**

FW-008, Page 1 of 2

Case Name:	Case Number:

b. ☐ The court **denies** your request and **will not waive or reduce** your fees and costs.

  (1) The reason for this denial is as follows:

    (a) ☐ Your request is incomplete, and you did not provide the information that the court requested *(specify items missing):*_____

    (b) ☐ You did not go to court on the hearing date to provide the information the court needed to make a decision.

    (c) ☐ The information you provide shows that you are not eligible for the fee waiver you requested because *(check all that apply):*

       i. ☐ Your income is too high.

       ii. ☐ Other *(explain):*_____

    (d) ☐ There is not enough evidence to support a fee waiver.

    (e) ☐ Other *(state reasons):*_____

  (2) ☐ You may pay some court fees and costs over time. You may make monthly payments of $_____ beginning *(date):*_____ and then payable on the 1st of each month after that, until the fees checked below are paid in full:

    (a) ☐ Filing fees.

    (b) ☐ Other *(describe):*_____

    You must pay all other court fees and costs as they are due.

c. ☐ The court **partially grants** your request so you can pay court fees without using money you need to pay for your household's basic needs. You are ordered to pay a portion of your fees, **as checked below.** The court only partially grants the request because *(state reasons for partial denial):*
_____
_____

  (1) ☐ You must pay_____% of your court fees.

  (2) ☐ The court waives some fees. The fees checked below are waived. You must pay all other court fees.

    ☐ Filing papers at superior court   ☐ Giving notice and certificates
    ☐ Sheriff's fee to give notice   ☐ Sending papers to another court department
    ☐ Court-appointed interpreter   ☐ Court-appointed interpreter fees for a witness
    ☐ Reporter's daily fee up to 60 days after order   ☐ Reporter's daily fees beyond the 60 days
    ☐ Jury fees and expenses   after initial order
    ☐ Court-appointed experts' fees   ☐ Fees for a peace officer to testify in court
    ☐ Making certified copies   ☐ Court fees for telephone hearings
    ☐ Other *(describe):*_____

  (3) ☐ Other *(specify):*_____

Warning! If b or c above are checked: You have **10 days** after the clerk gives notice of this order (see date below) to pay your fees as ordered, unless there is a later date for beginning payments in item b(2). If you do not pay, your court papers will not be processed. If the papers are a notice of appeal, your appeal may be dismissed.

Date:_____ ▶ _____
                           Signature of Judicial Officer

Clerk's Certificate of Service

I certify that I am not involved in this case and *(check one):* ☐ A certificate of mailing is attached.

☐ I handed a copy of this order to the party and attorney, if any, listed in ① and ②, at the court, on the date below.

☐ This order was mailed first class, postage paid, to the party and attorney, if any, at the addresses listed in ① and ②, from *(city):*_____, California on the date below.

Date:_____   Clerk, by _____, Deputy

NC-121

PETITIONER OR ATTORNEY *(Name, state bar number, and address)*:	FOR COURT USE ONLY

TELEPHONE NO.:   FAX NO. *(Optional)*:

E-MAIL ADDRESS *(Optional)*:

ATTORNEY FOR *(Name)*:

SUPERIOR COURT OF CALIFORNIA, COUNTY OF

STREET ADDRESS:

MAILING ADDRESS:

CITY AND ZIP CODE:

BRANCH NAME:

PETITION OF *(Names of each petitioner)*:

FOR CHANGE OF NAME

PROOF OF SERVICE OF ORDER TO SHOW CAUSE **BY** ☐ PERSONAL DELIVERY ☐ MAILING (OUTSIDE CALIFORNIA ONLY)	CASE NUMBER:

1. At the time of mailing or personal delivery, I was at least 18 years of age and **not a party** to this proceeding.

2. My residence or business address is *(specify)*:

3. I personally delivered or mailed a copy of the *Order to Show Cause for Change of Name* as follows *(complete either a or b)*:
   a. ☐ **Personal delivery.** I personally delivered a copy to the person served as follows:
       (1) Name of person served:
       (2) Address where delivered:

       (3) Date delivered:
       (4) Time delivered:

   b. ☐ **Mail.** I am a resident of or employed in the county where the mailing occurred.
       (1) I enclosed a copy in an envelope and mailed the sealed envelope to the person served by first-class mail, postage prepaid, return receipt requested, to the address outside of California listed below.
       (2) The envelope was addressed and mailed as follows:
           (a) Name of person served:
           (b) Address on envelope:

           (c) Date of mailing:
           (d) Place of mailing *(city and state)*:

I declare under penalty of perjury under the laws of the State of California that the foregoing is true and correct.

Date:

▶

_____   _____
(TYPE OR PRINT NAME OF DECLARANT)   (SIGNATURE OF DECLARANT)

Form Adopted for Mandatory Use Judicial Council of California NC-121 [New January 1, 2001]	**PROOF OF SERVICE OF ORDER TO SHOW CAUSE** **(Change of Name)**	**WEST GROUP** Official Publisher	Code of Civil Procedure, § 1277

Missing Parent Search Log

Date search initiated	Person performing the search	Person or entity contacted	Contact information	Results

MC-030

ATTORNEY OR PARTY WITHOUT ATTORNEY *(Name, State Bar number, and address):*

TELEPHONE NO.:   FAX NO. *(Optional):*

E-MAIL ADDRESS *(Optional):*

ATTORNEY FOR *(Name):*

SUPERIOR COURT OF CALIFORNIA, COUNTY OF

STREET ADDRESS:

MAILING ADDRESS:

CITY AND ZIP CODE:

BRANCH NAME:

PLAINTIFF/PETITIONER:

DEFENDANT/RESPONDENT:

DECLARATION

CASE NUMBER:

I declare under penalty of perjury under the laws of the State of California that the foregoing is true and correct.

Date:

_____
(TYPE OR PRINT NAME)

_____
(SIGNATURE OF DECLARANT)

☐ Attorney for ☐ Plaintiff ☐ Petitioner ☐ Defendant
☐ Respondent ☐ Other *(Specify):*

Form Approved for Optional Use
Judicial Council of California
MC-030 [Rev. January 1, 2006]

DECLARATION

Page 1 of 1

Index

1. Go to Nolo.com/newsletters to sign up for free newsletters and discounts on Nolo products.

   - **Nolo Briefs.** Our monthly email newsletter with great deals and free information.

   - **Nolo's Special Offer.** A monthly newsletter with the biggest Nolo discounts around.

   - **BizBriefs.** Tips and discounts on Nolo products for business owners and managers.

   - **Landlord's Quarterly.** Deals and free tips just for landlords and property managers, too.

2. Don't forget to check for updates at **Nolo.com.** Under "Products," find this book and click "Legal Updates."

Let Us Hear From You

3. Register your Nolo product and give us your feedback at Nolo.com/book-registration.

   - Once you've registered, you qualify for technical support if you have any trouble with a download or CD (though most folks don't).

   - We'll also drop you an email when a new edition of your book is released—and we'll send you a coupon for 15% off your next Nolo.com order!

NAME13

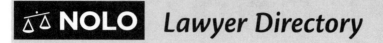

Find a Quality Attorney

- *Qualified lawyers*
- *In-depth profiles*
- *A pledge of respectful service*

When you want help with a serious legal problem, you don't want just any lawyer—you want an expert in the field who can give you and your family up-to-the-minute advice. You need a lawyer who has the experience and knowledge to answer your questions about personal injury, wills, family law, child custody, drafting a patent application or any other specialized legal area you are concerned with.

Nolo's Lawyer Directory is unique because it provides an extensive profile of every lawyer. You'll learn about not only each lawyer's education, professional history, legal specialties, credentials and fees, but also about their philosophy of practicing law and how they like to work with clients.

All lawyers listed in Nolo's directory are in good standing with their state bar association. Many will review Nolo documents, such as a will or living trust, for a fixed fee. They all pledge to work diligently and respectfully with clients—communicating regularly, providing a written agreement about how legal matters will be handled, sending clear and detailed bills and more.

www.nolo.com